Praise for *Engaging your Community through Active Strategic Marketing*

'An effective marketing strategy is vital in enabling library and information services to enhance their impact and engage existing and potential audiences. *Engaging your Community through Active Strategic Marketing* provides a comprehensive introduction on how to develop and implement your strategy, drawing on a useful collection of tips, tools and techniques. This practical guide is an invaluable resource for any information professional intending to measure and demonstrate the value of their marketing activities.'
Doug Knock, Library & Knowledge Services Manager, King's College Hospital NHS Foundation Trust

'In an age where libraries are competing with a wide range of entertainment and information facilities, a solid and strategic marketing plan can do wonders to engage existing clients and attract potential ones. This book is an accessible continuation of Terry's professional training methods in marketing specifically for libraries; he helps the library professional set up an effective marketing plan which moves away from the perhaps obvious system-based promotion style, to a targeted and individualistic method. I highly recommend this book to all library professionals who wish to give their library that extra edge.'
Cheryl Falzon, National Librarian and CEO, Malta Libraries

'As libraries respond to the disruption and challenge of technological change, the COVID-19 pandemic and financial uncertainty, *Engaging your Community through Active Strategic Marketing* stands as an invaluable resource.
Kendrick speaks to a bold ambition for libraries that roots its success in practical actions, with clear achievable outcomes. *Engaging Your Community* is a timely reminder that the services and institutions that endure are created in partnership with the communities they serve, placing community engagement and effective marketing at the heart of strategic planning for libraries. Alongside an accessible overview of key topics, *Engaging Your Community* includes suggestions for activities that will enable library and information professionals to build the "ongoing, engaging, meaningful conversations" with our communities that are essential to the future prosperity of our profession.'
Ed Jewell, Chief Librarian, Jersey Public Library

T0323459

'Terry's book *Engaging your Community through Active Strategic Marketing* is a great guide of step-by-step actions you can take to promote your library service in an increasingly crowded space for grabbing your users' attention. I began using Terry's tools and techniques after attending one of his workshops on library marketing a few years ago, and the cut-through we have achieved with our library marketing has been remarkable. This book will be a great asset to librarians and information professionals across all sectors who want to demonstrate their value in today's digital environment.'
Ella Hassett, Librarian, Arup

'Are you concerned that despite all your best efforts your library is still the "best kept secret?" Are you concerned that your library's marketing activities are not having the desired impact? Then Terry Kendrick's *Engaging your Community through Active Strategic Marketing* is just the book for you.

This sharply written and engaging book is full of useful tips and practical activities that will help you connect with your users, hone your library's marketing message and ultimately take your library's marketing to the next level, building and engaging your community along the way.'
Martin O'Connor, Academic Librarian, University College Cork Library, blogger for *Libfocus* and Chair of CONUL Communications and Outreach Group

Engaging your Community through Active Strategic Marketing

Every purchase of a Facet book helps to fund CILIP's advocacy, awareness and accreditation programmes for information professionals.

Engaging your Community through Active Strategic Marketing:

A practical guide for librarians and information professionals

Terry Kendrick

facet
publishing

Published by Facet Publishing,
c/o British Library, 96 Euston Road, London NW1 2DB
www.facetpublishing.co.uk

Facet Publishing is wholly owned by CILIP: the Library
and Information Association.

British Library Cataloguing in Publication Data
A catalogue record for this book is available from the British Library.

ISBN 978-1-78330-383-0 (paperback)
ISBN 978-1-78330-384-7 (hardback)
ISBN 978-1-78330-385-4 (PDF)
ISBN 978-1-78330-519-3 (EPUB)

First published 2021

Typeset from author's files by Flagholme Publishing Services in
10/13 pt Palatino Linotype and Open Sans.
Printed and made in Great Britain by CPI Group (UK) Ltd, Croydon, CR0 4YY.

Contents

VIII ENGAGING YOUR COMMUNITY THROUGH ACTIVE STRATEGIC MARKETING

Figures

Tables

Introduction

Perhaps more than ever before, library staff – regardless of sector – seek to engage with those who will shape the library's destiny. Users should be engaged when they visit libraries. Library staff need to understand why some people do not use libraries and draw them closer. Stakeholders such as administrators of funding bodies need to be engaged to ensure alignment of library values, vision and mission with the wider organisational goals.

This book, based on modern engagement and marketing planning principles, has been written as a practical guide to support staff in libraries of all kinds in their efforts to encourage users, non-users and other stakeholders to engage with library services.

Successful engagement arises from a well-managed combination of outreach, advocacy, campaign marketing, user experience, customer service and external relations. Strategic marketing planning offers a process to manage and deliver the major benefits of each of these in search of authentic and sustained engagement with library communities, whether geographical or communities of need or interest.

Although some of the terminology characteristic of these disciplines has been retained, the overriding concern has been to use easy to understand language and avoid jargon wherever possible. Similarly, where there are models that simplify some of the concepts discussed in the book, they have been adapted to have specific relevance for libraries.

Examples given in this book are drawn mainly from public, academic, health services and corporate libraries to explain and inspire.

Terry Kendrick
December 2020

The need for a professional approach to engagement

We live in a busy, noisy, unpredictable world where even our cherished beliefs and values are under review. From the big issues around how we should be governed, through social issues of support and fairness, to the less fundamental, but still disorienting, shift in the patterns of how and where we buy things, we are living through a period of seemingly accelerating change.

Libraries are inevitably caught up in this swirling change and their values are being challenged in all sectors for relevance, need and value for money. There is an imperative for librarians to engage deeply with their users, potential users and other stakeholders, encouraging them to use library services. These are exciting times for libraries with this deeper engagement revealing new opportunities and highlighting the continuing relevance of existing well-established library values and services.

Defining engagement and strategic marketing

Engagement can be defined and measured by how involved people are with the library and how sustained their connections are over time. The process of attracting users, potential users and other stakeholders involves leading them into an ongoing relationship with the library. This may begin by encouraging library use but can, as engagement deepens, develop into co-creation of services.

Sometimes this involvement and connection arises naturally due to an apparent good fit and understanding between the library ethos and what the users, potential users and other stakeholders want, and expect, from library service. At other times potential fit should be investigated, understood, developed, managed and monitored. This book suggests practical approaches to engagement through strategic marketing planning.

Although engagement is most frequently discussed in relation to public, academic and health library services it is a topic that is key to successful development and delivery of services in all library and information sectors. The following chapters outline practical tools and techniques to ensure successful, meaningful, engagement regardless of library context. Underpinning the exploration of strategic marketing for engagement will be a nod to the related concepts of outreach, advocacy, campaign marketing, customer service and external relations. All of these, if well managed, contribute to the potential for deep engagement.

For the purpose of this book strategic marketing in a library and information context can be defined as:

> An ongoing, engaging, meaningful conversation with users, potential users and other stakeholders to understand the appropriate configuration of valuable products and services, which can then be moulded into mutually beneficial segment-specific winning offers that are subsequently communicated, implemented, evaluated and monitored.

Although long, it is worth memorising this definition to use as a check for your marketing activities. If your project or campaign is not addressing at least one part of this definition (and preferably several) then it is unlikely that you will be encouraging engagement or, indeed, undertaking strategic marketing.

The definition stresses the importance of relationship marketing and an overall strategic planning process while clearly including significant items from related concepts such as outreach (e.g. the ongoing engaging conversations), advocacy (e.g. communicating and championing the value of the library offer), customer service (e.g. effective, careful, sensitive delivery of offers to provide a positive and consistent user experience) and external relations (e.g. the importance of wider stakeholder groups).

Tactical marketing activities and campaigns should be based on winning offers that are more attractive than relevant competitive offers, relevant, timely and engaging. The library should not be seen as simply the source of 'one more message'. Sitting back on a wonderful product with a hope that someone – key funding stakeholders and potential library users – will spot your wonderfulness is not likely to be an effective development strategy. In our noisy times the fight for attention is severe and brutal. Being the best kept secret is dangerous positioning. The library offer clearly needs to be attractive, not merely well stated and communicated.

Before moving on to discuss the tools and techniques of effective marketing for engagement in libraries let us take a moment to recognise why this is so important a topic today. An increased professionalism around engagement and strategic marketing is required for many reasons, which are discussed below:

- Library and information services are often losing market share.
- Library and information units need to be relevant to a significant proportion of their potential user population.
- Effective marketing strategy is no longer simply about publicising and promoting existing services.
- Sometimes users cannot articulate their future needs well or have a limited understanding of library capabilities.
- Those who fund libraries need to know how well funds allocated to the library are being used to meet the information or leisure requirements of its clientele.
- Brand and image are important to many.
- Some library and information units have been disappointed by the outcomes of their seemingly ineffective marketing activities.
- Library and information units must satisfy users otherwise there is very little chance of those users continuing to use and truly engage with them.

Library and information services are, in most sectors and contexts, in fast growing information and leisure markets and losing market share. The services and products that library and information units offer are increasingly recognised as important by a range of people. At the same time there are ever more alternative – often seemingly more engaging – ways to access relevant services and products, each with its own distinctive approach. This is a fundamental double issue that must be addressed – library and information services should be experiencing a very successful era but this is not always the case. An increased professionalism to analyse marketplaces and develop effective general and marketing strategies is required if an appropriate share of this marketplace is to be engaged. Strategic marketing planning is an important tool to address this issue.

Library and information units should be relevant to a significant proportion of a library's potential user population. Library and information managers need to present their services as an indispensable, or at least very valuable, part of the daily life of their users. Where services are publicly funded, such as public libraries, a plausible and evidenced claim must be made that users' lives are constantly improved at least in line with current local authority priorities. A deep understanding of users and the value provided for them is part of the goal and outcome for strategic marketing. Empathy and engagement are key drivers of success.

Given the changing nature of our uncertain environments, effective marketing strategy is no longer simply about publicising and promoting existing services. It is vital to know when it is time to innovate to ensure continued relevance. Innovation requires feedback from engaged users and other stakeholders. Well-designed marketing planning activities are an important source of this detailed, structured and regular feedback. Innovation is not simply about asking users what they want.

Innovators recognise that sometimes users cannot articulate their future needs well or they simply articulate them in the context of their, possibly limited, understanding of library capabilities. Those managing strategic marketing look at a whole range of scenarios and go beyond simply building on existing strengths to ensure the library service anticipates as well as reflects. Anticipation of changing user needs requires more than simply a survey – it requires deep user engagement if you are to understand the implications of the information collected in surveys. Without this how can a library establish which innovations are most likely to help users achieve their goals?

Those who fund libraries should know how well funds allocated to the library are being used to meet the information or leisure needs of its clientele. Those managing funding bodies should be notified of costs and outcomes to ensure their continued commitment and support. Strategic marketing reveals the combinations of products and services that deliver the most value for the investment in the service.

Brand and image are important to many. Do your potential users want to be associated with you or do you not fit with the set of people and organisations that they wish to be seen with? Strategic marketing can disentangle this issue and provide users and other stakeholders with powerful ways in which to engage with the library or information service brand.

Some library and information units have been disappointed by the outcomes of their seemingly ineffective marketing activities. Often this is because their efforts have been very much based on broadcasting information and not focused on how the library helps individual groups of users, potential users or other stakeholders get to where they intend to go. In an age where attention spans are short, keep marketing messages interesting rather than simply informational.

Library and information units must have satisfied users otherwise there is very little chance of repeated use and true engagement. Ongoing conversations as part of marketing activities will often include satisfaction surveys. However, managers of strategic marketing recognise that simple high satisfaction scores, while necessary for potential repeat use, will not automatically be sufficient to ensure repeat use. Despite good service, in our consumer lives we are often tempted by enticing, attractive messages of others and this is no different in the library and information world where the opportunities to satisfy a leisure or information need are many and varied. A professional approach to marketing library and information units will not simply be messaging and tracking satisfaction but will constantly attempt to keep open, involving, engaging, conversations with users. Such open conversations can help ensure some degree of co-creation with users.

Outline of this book

These reasons to employ a professional strategic marketing approach to developing engagement in library and information units provide a good case for investing thinking time in devising marketing strategy. First steps in marketing often bring dramatic insights rather than dramatic results but learning loops increase the power of subsequent marketing activities. The strategic marketing success this book aims to encourage is more easily discussed than implemented. The final chapter of this book (Chapter 12) suggests some key practical activities you can deploy to give your strategy development and implementation activities the best chance of success in engaging library users, non-users and other stakeholders.

Before reaching Chapter 12 this book will outline the strategic marketing planning process and its application in user engagement (Chapter 2); look at the role of ambition in successful marketing planning (Chapter 3); offer advice and techniques for understanding users and potential users of the service (Chapter 4); look at how this understanding can help identify engaging value propositions for specific groups of users (Chapter 5); uncover the best ways to involve, engage and generate support from important stakeholder groups (Chapter 6); examine strategic marketing choices about existing or new products and services to specific groups of users or non-users (Chapter 7); develop engaging marketing messages for users, potential users and other stakeholders (Chapter 8); identify and employ effective marketing channels to get the messages out (Chapter 9); highlight the pivotal role of digital marketing in engagement (Chapter 10); evaluate and report on the response to your marketing and engagement activities (Chapter 11).

Throughout the book there are tools and techniques to support your planning activities, and suggestions of good practice, though be wary of simply copying another library and information unit's marketing activities. What works for them may not work for you.

2

Strategic marketing planning for engagement

Although some people naturally engage with library and information services many others do not. The 'non-naturals' need to be persuaded that the service is worth investing the time and effort for the value it can bring to them. A series of one-off high profile outreach, advocacy or marketing activities is, of itself, unlikely to be powerful enough to persuade the 'non-naturals' to engage in any meaningful way. Plan in the short term (one year), medium term (three years) and long term (five to ten years). Given the high degree of uncertainty in the modern world the long-term plans are likely to be little more than strategic intent but the one- to three-year plans require detail, focus and commitment if engagement is to be sparked and developed.

Sometimes library and information staff are disappointed by the results of their engagement activities. In an attempt to encourage engagement public librarians may have dressed up as cartoon characters, academic librarians may have exalted the virtues of new online database subscriptions, and company librarians may have offered drop-in sessions with coffee. All these activities have good engagement principles driving them but the results of such activities are often seen to be disappointing.

This disappointment is not explained by a lack of staff creativity or professionalism. In recent years library and information staff have invested much time and thought in acquiring techniques for, and skills in, outreach, advocacy, customer service, external relations and marketing. Library and information staff are reflective, creative, hard working, and ever alert to potential library applications in new technologies and on social media platforms. In addition, they have a genuine desire to make a difference and build relationships with users and potential users. The source of this sometimes frustrating lack of engagement by library users and other stakeholders can often be traced to a lack of detailed strategic planning for engagement.

While it is common to see excellent 'one-off' events and promotions in libraries it is less common, though far from unknown, to see adherence to a full three- or even one-year detailed action plan to build relationships and develop a conversation with users and other stakeholders. Engagement is more than the result of implementing a quick series of marketing communications effectively. Quick wins are important to sustain staff morale but they are not the essence of sustained engagement. And given the distracting levels of uncertainty in the world it is often difficult to commit to the next six months, never mind a full one-year tactical plan or three-year strategic plan.

Strategic marketing planning for engagement requires very detailed knowledge of users and their hopes, fears, needs, wants, attitudes, behaviours and values. Library staff should be clear what offers they can make to users and have confidence they can deliver them in ways that resonate with users, and can attract their attention. This thinking should be made practical through a three-year strategic marketing and engagement plan supported by a detailed first-year plan. The engagement, or strategic marketing, plan needs to be discussed and updated regularly during the annual cycle of library planning meetings.

The approach to planning for engagement can be one of two approaches, or both:

- user engagement with library values and preferred outcomes
- library engagement with user values and preferred outcomes.

Effective strategic planning requires both of these two approaches to be considered in tandem. To look at only one of these two is to miss the opportunity to create fit between users and libraries. Fit is essential for engagement, which is a complex mix of processes and outcomes that need to be managed in an integrated and strategic approach, as set out in Table 2.1 opposite.

When developing a strategic marketing plan within this complex mix of inputs and outputs it becomes clear very quickly that the information needed to drive things forward to a successful engagement can only be provided by consulting a wide range of stakeholders. This is not an activity that is best undertaken quickly within the chief librarian's office with a couple of token staff and users as inputs to the decision-making process. There has to be wide consultation and involvement to achieve meaningful engagement.

The preferred outcome for engagement is involved users, who interact with the library, are engrossed in its services, feel comfortable in interactions, and care enough to keep the library aware of users' changing needs through

Table 2.1 *Engagement processes and outcomes*

Engagement process or outcome	Why this is important for engagement
Co-creation of value and shared purposeful outcomes that matter to the library, users and other stakeholders	To be engaged you need to feel that you matter to the service provider, and their products and services have been created not just for you but also with you
Collaboration on specific projects together	Both sides need to feel that they are working together on common projects if there is to be a close relationship
Opportunity to interact easily with the library service	To be engaged there must be clear lines of communication and opportunities to interact as often as required or desired by those you wish to engage with you
Library responsiveness to contacts and comment	It is unlikely that anyone will engage with a service that is unresponsive to requests for information, comments or complaints
Shared development of brand values experience and consequent loyalty	Positive responses to your messages will come when people respect your purpose and values; they need not buy in to absolutely every element of your purpose but there must be enough shared vision and purpose there to bring stakeholders together rather than divide them; any consequent loyalty should be both ways – not only should users and other stakeholders be loyal to the library but the library should exhibit loyalty towards them
Development of emotional as well as rational relationship	Engagement is rarely simply a rational response; positive feelings and reactions to the library's message are important to draw people closer and into more meaningful conversations
Rapport between library and its stakeholders	Ease of communication and an underlying positivity in discussions will act as an enabler for engagement
Establishment of trust both in privacy and readiness; willingness and ability to deliver the promised services	Unfulfilled promises are unlikely to encourage engagement; insensitive use of personal data is likely to be seen as a lack of integrity within the service and distance rather than engage users and other stakeholders
Demonstrable commitment of library staff and stakeholders to stay close to each other	Engagement is unlikely where service is inconsistent and not backed by evidenced commitment

formal or informal channels. In addition they feel happy to be associated with the library brand and feel some degree of loyalty towards it, at least in part because they perceive the service to be of high quality. They trust librarians to be looking after their best interests. In essence the objective of engagement activity is the library staff working collaboratively with users to address common issues. Engagement is often, but not always, the outcome of great user experience.

Engagement is the preferred outcome and not easily achieved by either the library or the user. There are far too many complex variables to be managed to create guaranteed outcomes. Strategic marketing planning processes have tools to manage at least some of these engagement objectives in various combinations. This will always be part of a journey; a successful engagement project is never ending, and needs to be maintained and developed through an ongoing plan. One round of planning, even with all boxes ticked, will not be sufficient.

All strategic marketing planning activity for engagement is essentially within a process and context of co-creation and delivery of value. This context is constantly changing so any strategic marketing plan should be hospitable to changes and emerging trends and requirements. This requires a deep relationship between users and the library. Library staff must understand the differences between users rather than simply look for their unifying characteristics. They need to understand their life cycles and life events, which may determine what they require from the library service (more on this in Chapter 4). In summary, the library or information service needs to be opportunistic within a general strategic intent and plan, flexible enough to withstand change and humble enough to recognise that change is necessary.

Strategic marketing planning processes are unlikely to engage all people to the same extent. There needs to be a segmentation that results in different expectations around degrees of relationship and engagement. Beware a small number of vocal and highly engaged users who potentially wield disproportionate influence. They may not be representative of the majority of users, or priority users, as outlined in policy documents, so be wary of allowing them to co-create products and services. Remember, you are the library managers who have to allocate resources fairly. Do not willingly devolve your management responsibilities to vocal stakeholders.

Identifying planning goals and processes to achieve them

You are now ready to identify your planning goals and consider processes to achieve them. To gain a detailed understanding of users, ask:

- Who am I seeking to engage with the library service? Is it realistic to expect potential library users to engage?
- In what ways do I want them to engage? Will they engage that way?
- How will I move potential library users towards the level of engagement I, and/or they, desire?

- What tactics, technologies, tools and techniques will support engagement?

It is likely that if you say it is your goal to engage deeply with all then success is far from assured. You will almost certainly not have enough resource in money or time to deliver such an overly ambitious undertaking. In addition, not all user groups and other stakeholders will want to engage deeply with the library service. Your strategic marketing plan has to choose key stakeholder groups and focus on having impact within that. You may choose several groups or one and base your actions on this choice. Although you are driving the planning for engagement you may be able, as the saying goes, to lead the horses (potential users) to water but you may not be able to make them drink (engage). To make them drink you may need to make them thirsty first or at least approach them when they are thirsty. Be aware that there may be ways in which users would like to engage that you either have not thought of or do not especially wish to encourage. This needs to be managed sensitively.

To undertake strategic marketing planning to underpin effective engagement requires a number of steps to be followed regardless of library context. There are many books on strategic marketing planning from which you could derive an appropriate logic for your process. Here is a logical sequence of actions to undertake when creating a strategic marketing plan for engagement:

- *Think about your purpose and values.* Be clear what your library stands for and inform all stakeholders, from users to funding bodies.
- *Agree your ambition, goals and objectives for engaging users.* Be clear what level of achievement and engagement the library is planning for.
- *Analyse all stakeholders through segmentation.* Consider potential and current users, funders, champions, staff and others. This will help you choose which engagement activities have the greatest chance of success, or where important engagement activities may need more than usual levels of support to be effective.
- *Carry out a value analysis.* This helps you find out why potential users may engage with the library and think about why the library would invest in the time to attract specific groups of users.
- *Carry out a SWOT exercise looking at your strengths, weaknesses, opportunities and threats.* This helps you clarify where efforts are most likely to be most successful and where significant improvements need to be made if you are to engage with some of your users and other stakeholders.

■ *Consider your choices and resource allocation.* Include choice of outreach and advocacy partners. You need to prioritise your efforts to ensure there are enough resources deployed in specific activities to ensure success.

■ *Develop your offer.* Having undertaken all the thinking and analysis suggested above, your offer to the chosen identified groups must be the winning offer not simply another good offer they receive in their busy day.

■ *Develop your message.* It is crucial to explain your offer to specific users or other stakeholder segments to engage with them. Create a set of messages for different stakeholder categories rather than a one size fits all message.

■ *Deliver your message.* You might do this through action plans, user experience monitoring and service levels. If you are successful in engaging users and then do not deliver what was promised all your efforts are likely to have been in vain. During this stage of engagement planning the choice of marketing and other communication channels is very important. Your message must be distributed through reliable, appropriate and authentic channels.

■ *Create an action plan.* Turn all the planning work so far into manageable related chunks that together over a year (tactical programmes) and three years (roll out of strategy) implement all objectives derived from the analysis and priorities. All actions should have a resource allocation, and a clear indication of when they will be completed and who is responsible for completing them.

■ *Evaluate your impact and success.* Close monitoring will ensure that you identify strategies and action that have been effective and those that have not been so effective. This is the basis for discussion at each regular service management meeting. A next steps approach at these meetings is important to ensure that there is an ongoing process of engagement.

Clearly, although this is a logical sequence there may be a number of loops in this list; earlier stages may be revisited as new information or experiences arise. This is not simply a 'tick box' activity but far more iterative. Once a strategic marketing plan is in place an alert management team should not be afraid to amend it within the broader strategic intent. It is unlikely that any plan will go exactly to schedule. It may be appropriate to have the plan as a shareable amendable online document rather than in print. Think of your plan as a roadmap hospitable to adjustments.

The engagement story

Another way of conceptualising the plan for engagement is to turn the process into a story based on all the analysis you make in subsequent chapters of this book, as set out in Table 2.2. Simply complete the sentence that is started in the first column in the second column. Feel free to amend the storyline to include other items important to you.

Table 2.2 *The engagement story*

Element of engagement story	Your story
We aim to (purpose and values)	
achieving the following engagement goals and ambition	
within the following timescale	
To achieve this we will focus on the following user, potential user and stakeholder groups	
who we are confident of providing these services, which will be of value to them	
Our analysis shows we have a good chance of providing winning offers (compared with their alternative sources of this value). We have the following strengths to maximise opportunities for engagement	
and have the following strategies to make our weaknesses less limiting and our threats deflected	
We have identified the following allies and other stakeholders to support us in our engagement project and will ensure they are considered in our management of the project	
Reflecting on all this we have created the following winning offers for our key chosen stakeholders (user groups and other stakeholder groups)	
Our engagement activities as part of this plan have been budgeted and funding secured to the following level	
We have developed messages, by group, as follows	
and have tested them for effectiveness and appropriateness on potential recipients by	
Our message and other action plans have been developed around the following delivery channels in the following timescales	
We are confident that when the messages are received we can deliver as promised and the user's experience will be good to excellent because we have the following monitoring in place	
Our approach to measuring engagement success and deciding next steps is	

You may look at this story template and think that it looks complicated and time-consuming. You may ask whether the logic and the story is worth all the effort. Why not just do a 'flashy' marketing campaign with great production values, buzz words and strap line standing back awaiting the rush of new users with other stakeholders beating on our doors, desperate to offer us more financial support? Why do we not simply advocate the value of libraries and undertake outreach events to get the message out? True engagement requires significant, sustained, co-ordinated effort over time if we are not to be disappointed by our efforts.

The important point in any strategic marketing planning process is that it is adapted to your particular context. You will see from this that wider reading shows these ideas to be the core of all strategic marketing planning but here the process is considered from a library and information services point of view. You should think even more about this and adapt it to the important things within your specific library context. Involve as many people as you can in this process and make it fun. If you cannot engage your staff in this process what are the chances of you being able to engage those users, potential users or other stakeholders you dearly want to care about what you are doing?

It is time to move on to look in practical detail at the thinking, reflection and analysis needed at various parts of the planning process outlined above. Chapter 3 guides you to create an overarching ambition for your engagement activities; Chapter 4 provides the context and toolkit for understanding users and the wider marketplace for the services they need and want; Chapter 5 analyses what value is and how understanding it will drive your particular engagement activities; Chapter 6 considers how wider stakeholder groups can be engaged and support your activities with specific user or potential user groups; Chapter 7 gives you a rationale for making priorities and choices for engagement activities; Chapter 8 advises on how to make your messages for chosen groups to be engaging rather than simply informational; Chapter 9 outlines your potential range of message delivery channels with advice on which are more likely to be engaging than others; Chapter 10 emphasises the important role of digital channels, such as social media, and advises on how to be truly engaging in such busy and noisy media; Chapter 11 suggests ways to evaluate the response to your engagement activities; Chapter 12 offers practical tips on how to ensure your engagement efforts have the best chance of success, as they will face many constraints and barriers.

Have you memorised the definition of strategic marketing as set out in Chapter 1 yet? It is worth memorising the definition of strategic marketing set out in Chapter 1 as an anchor and overview for all the very detailed planning engagement activity we are about to undertake. Take a glass or cup of your favourite beverage with a favourite nibble and spend some time reflecting on this chapter before rushing into the practical activity chapters ahead. Have you got the logic of your engagement story clear? We all like to be activity driven but without undertaking planning activity within the logic of this chapter you may end up as one of those disappointed by their engagement activities.

3

Ambition: the basis for all activity

Action is essential when developing a plan to engage with users and other stakeholders but this action needs to have a context. It is not sufficient simply to offer a programme of generally positive activities with the hope that in some mystical way such initiatives will generate deep engagement and associated positive actions among users, potential users and other stakeholders.

Every type of library and information unit benefits from devising a clear statement of ambition to keep it close to users, potential users and the expectations and requirements of the funding bodies and other stakeholders. Reflection on the ideas discussed in Chapter 2 will help you clarify what you mean by engagement, but how will you know if the action plans in your strategic marketing and engagement plan have been successful? Simply completing tasks may not achieve desired outcomes. A statement of ambition gives you a baseline from which to judge success or otherwise, and these statements are particularly useful in managing relationships with funding bodies. In an amended form, they can potentially inspire users, potential users and other stakeholders.

For instance, public librarians need to show how they are contributing to the priorities of the councils that fund them, company librarians should align with the goals of the wider organisation (which are often related to delivering profit or a culture of innovation but may have wider social concerns as well) and health librarians need to show how they contribute to the delivery of a high level of patient care at reasonable cost. Academic librarians should show how they contribute to successful student experiences and outcomes and support faculty contributions to knowledge through research. In each of these, and other cases, this gives context for what the library and information service will encourage users and other stakeholders to engage with.

Perhaps the most overt application of ambition has been made in public libraries. In the UK, for instance, in 2018 the Department for Digital, Culture, Media & Sport published *Libraries Deliver* (DCMS, 2018). In Scotland, the Carnegie UK Trust was commissioned to write a national strategy for public libraries, *Ambition and Opportunity* (Carnegie UK Trust, 2015). In the health sector, the website of NHS Health Education England sets out its qualitative and quantitative objectives towards fulfilling ambition:

> Healthcare library and knowledge services underpin education, lifelong learning, research and evidence-based practice. Our ambition is to extend this role so that healthcare knowledge services become the integral part of informed decision-making and innovation.
>
> We published Knowledge for Healthcare, sharing our vision that NHS bodies, their staff, learners, patients and the public use the right knowledge and evidence, at the right time, in the right place, enabling high-quality decision-making, learning, research and innovation to achieve excellent healthcare and health improvement.
>
> Health Education England, 2020

In some contexts library staff might use the terms vision, mission and values instead of ambition.

Vision, mission and values

In many libraries ambitions arise from a continuum of vision–mission values. A vision statement is a qualitative statement of a library's driving aspirations of what it hopes to achieve or to become. The vision statement and mission statement are occasionally confused, and many organisations use the terms interchangeably. However, they each have a different purpose. The vision statement describes where the organisation wants to be in the future; the mission statement describes what the organisation needs to do now to achieve its vision. The values statement outlines what the organisation believes in and how people in the organisation are expected to behave – with each other, users, suppliers and other stakeholders.

An academic library might have the following progression of vision, mission and values:

- *vision*: 'to lead, learn and inspire success'
- *mission*: 'to generate regional economic growth and social well-being by providing skills and education for individuals, employers and the wider community'
- *values*: 'to inspire, innovate, trust, respect and succeed'.

These values are very important in creating some degree of engagement with users, potential users and other stakeholders. Who wants to engage with the uninspired, stale, untrustworthy, disreputable and unsuccessful?

Sometimes the ambition can be derived from qualitative strategic priorities or strategic intent as in the National Library of the Netherlands' four priorities: 'Setting the written word to work in society; taking care of the written word; organising an infrastructure for the written word; developing our organisation and our networks' (Koninklijke Bibliotheek, 2018).

A thorough statement of ambition combines purpose (vision, mission, values) and the level of activity and quantified outcomes expected from pursuing that purpose over a stated period of time. It can be simply a statement of the direction of travel with no end point, but if it needs to gain support from those funding the library, it is wise to include a combination of qualitative purpose and quantitative milestones. For instance, in a company library, a simple statement that the library has the ambition to become 'the source of choice for information requirements within our organisation' can be significantly improved by giving some indication of the level of activity and outcomes needed to meet this ambition. Statements of ambition should not be glib.

As noted above, library ambition can be thought of as having two key dimensions:

- overall purpose within library values (qualitative ambition)
- required, or anticipated, results (quantitative ambition).

Without reflection on, and alignment with, these two dimensions library engagement activities can drift and lose focus. When considering potential engagement activity question your choices by asking, 'How will this help us to move towards achieving our engagement ambition?' when considering purpose and results. Without some degree of understanding and clarity of ambition how will you be able to judge the success or otherwise of your engagement activities?

What does engagement mean in practical quantifiable terms? How would we spot it and measure its progress? By counting how many positive comments we get? Or how many offers of help we get for activities? Or how many champions we can call on to support us in times of need? Do we define ambition simply by issuing a certain number of books by a certain time? How many visits by when? How many website hits by when? How many Facebook likes? How many comments on our digital posts? Without some degree of understanding of the levels of return on marketing investment to be achieved it is difficult to devise an effective and persuasive engagement-driven marketing plan.

Here are a few examples of potential engagement, strategic and qualitative ambitions within various types of library:

- We want to be seen as a fun and relaxed place to visit.
- We want to be seen as the heart of the community.
- We want to be the first thing that comes to mind when a member of our user community needs information of any sort.
- Within our organisation we aim to be the most trusted source of external information.
- We want to create positive associations regarding the library as an institution.

These are examples of tactical level and quantitative ambitions:

- We want the number of visitors to the physical library to increase by 50% within the next three years.
- We want to have at least 1,000 followers on Twitter within the next two years.
- We want to print three positive stories in the company newsletter by the end of this year.

There are practical implications of quantified ambitions. Consider three possible quantified engagement ambitions of a public library authority over the next year:

- *Scenario 1*: maintain comments on our social media posts at 20 per month
- *Scenario 2*: double comments on our social media posts to 40 per month
- *Scenario 3*: increase comments on our social media posts to 200 per month.

The advantages of such quantifications are:

- to encourage you to make sense of what a level of engagement means to you; in the example here engagement is seen as something much more than awareness but a conversation
- by quantifying your key indicators to enable you to see the difficulty of the task you are facing and focus your thoughts on creating strategies and actions sufficiently robust to achieve something meaningful
- if there is an intention simply to increase comments by 100% from a low base (scenario 2) this will require a different marketing and engagement strategy plan and resource than if the intention is to increase comments significantly (scenario 3).

The strategic plan takes the ambition and provides the roadmap for the next three years of working towards that ambition. A supporting one-year action plan (the first year of the detailed implementation of the three-year plan) provides the specific actions needed to proceed. Such a seemingly rigid plan should remain open to opportunism but within the overall ambition. Actions that do not clearly have the potential to help the library fulfil its ambition are not to be encouraged.

There are some difficult variables to measure but which may well identify high levels of engagement, for example sentiment, user referrals, advocacy on social media. These types of variables can be used to identify how many users and other stakeholders are engaged and committed to the library beyond simply using it on appropriate occasions.

There is more detail on measuring and evaluating these type of variables and the actions we do to influence them in Chapter 11, but at this stage in the process you should have a relatively clear idea of which engagement variables are the most important to your library service. At the ambition level you need only have a few key variables within your statement of ambition, which will form your context to guide decisions and activities, offering the focus around which staff can operate.

How to write a statement of ambition for your library

An effective statement of engagement ambition combines qualitative and quantitative elements and should be developed with input from all levels of staff, led by the senior management team and with commitment from the library funding body.

The statement should not be so long as to confuse the context for marketing planning and not so short as to be simply a slogan. Although a slogan (e.g. 'we aim to engage with people to help them have more fulfilling lives' or 'we intend to fully engage with health service staff to deliver better patient care and outcomes' or 'we will engage with all departments of our company to deliver profitable quality products' or 'we will engage with students to help them achieve better exam results and with academics to support them in writing better academic papers') sets the atmosphere, and can be very useful to attract attention if well devised, without some quantification it does not provide the practical basis for realistic short- to medium-term planning.

The statement should be written around your specific library service and not just summarise other library ambition statements giving different quantitative data.

There is no ideal size for a statement of ambition but keep it succinct. It can be a challenge to be ambitious in both vision, mission values and quantitative objectives. Avoid making two initial 'big mistakes':

- *Only one person writing it.* You may be able to write it yourself but you will not be able to deliver it yourself no matter how good a library leader and manager you are.
- *Trying to please everyone with one statement.* For example, using words that funding bodies will understand but which do not engage staff. If you need to reflect the different vocabularies of different stakeholders then you need to write a series of consistent statements to reflect these differences. This is perfectly acceptable in the process of creating ambition and reflects a key marketing concept – segmentation. Each stakeholder group will have slightly different reasonable expectations of the library and each should be in no doubt as to where you are taking the library service *in their terms.*

When devising quantified engagement objectives avoid making further big mistakes:

- *Having too many objectives to manage.* Beware of counting things which have no real impact on engagement levels or the thinking that 'we may as well count them while we are counting the key things'.
- *Not knowing where you will find support.* Beware not being clear which user groups and other stakeholders are likely to support the aim of achieving the quantified engagement objectives.
- *Having unrealistic expectations.* The results of many marketing activities cannot be observed immediately but only over a period of several years if they are sustained. Remember that engagement happens over time and to label a user who has used the library only once as engaged may in your definition be technically correct, but the single visit by this user cannot be said to demonstrate that you have attracted more potential users to truly engage with the library. Most objectives involving engagement cannot be met quickly.
- *Having no idea of what has worked in the past and how well.* Although the future will not be the same as the past it is very useful to have an indication of the amount of return received for specific types of past marketing activity. This will help staff to set realistic expectations in the plan. In some marketing planning such as user retention activities it soon becomes evident what will work and what will not.

Once you have written the statement of ambition consider whether it is sufficient by asking these questions:

■ Can you see how it directly links to what you should do next? Does it provide a practical context for your forthcoming marketing plan? If the statement of ambition feels motherhood then staff are unlikely to be convinced and you will not be able to create a crisp, inspiring marketing plan which unites the staff in pursuit of your engagement ambition.
■ Would all stakeholders understand it, feel inspired by it and get behind it? If you feel that engagement would vary by type of stakeholder, consider writing separate, consistent, ambitions for each stakeholder category. Marketing is about communicating messages as much as it is about anything and if you need to create different messages to engage different stakeholder groups then do so.
■ Does it create a 'buzz' and positive emotions and feelings? Remember, engagement arises from rational and emotional reflection. Can that 'buzz' and emotion be marketed and communicated? For marketing and engagement planning you should use the statement of ambition, not just present it to the funding body and maybe put it on the wall as a potentially futile attempt to engage staff.
■ Is the ambition likely to sustain activities for at least two strategic planning periods (e.g. six years?). Given the inevitable amount of change that library markets experience will it still look appropriate in five years' time? Can it remain a unifying force for staff through the inevitable changes in users' and other stakeholders' needs and expectations? If you cannot be confident of this then prepare to have a service that increasingly does not make sense to all stakeholders as you try constantly to realign it around ever changing priorities.
■ Will it survive the legitimate distractions posed by funding body committee members who have specific agendas?
■ Is it engaging, succinct, exciting, believable, robust and achievable?

Table 3.1 on the next page gives a template to help you craft your statement of ambition, initially setting out your overarching vision and values, then your qualitative and quantitative ambitions for the planning period.

A marketing plan is likely to be little more than an advertising and promotional plan rather than a plan for engagement if you:

■ do not know what your library stands for and believes in
■ do not know the principles you operate by and how you will treat those who come in contact with the library

Table 3.1 *The statement of ambition*

Overarching vision (qualitative statement)		
Overarching values (qualitative statement)		
Group to be engaged	Qualitative ambition during planning period	Quantitative ambition during planning period
Users		
Potential users		
Stakeholders (funding and governance)		
Allies (clear supporters or champions)		
Other stakeholders (e.g. suppliers)		
Library staff		

- are not excited about what you are doing and lack passion for your library service provision
- are out of touch with your users and other stakeholders, the feelings of your employees, and your funding body's interests and concerns
- have little grasp of the quantifiable engagement performance metrics and how they have been influenced by specific marketing initiatives in the past
- do not recognise the fundamental part staff play in engaging stakeholders.

It is possible that your first draft of ambition will contain some almost heroic levels of ambition and activity that will prove difficult to achieve. Do not expect to feel that you have to get it completely right at the beginning of your marketing planning process. Initially spend no more than a half-day on creating the ambition – you may well want to change it as the early planning decisions for your library are made. It is not unusual for an initial statement to prove over-optimistic when later research shows either a smaller size of opportunity than originally envisaged or a more difficult user or stakeholder group to engage with than first assumed. Marketing planning is an iterative process. So is engagement.

Once your engagement ambition has been devised you will quickly see that it will keep your focus on the core things you wish to achieve. Having understood the importance of creating your statement of ambition it is time to move on to understand users, potential users and other stakeholders and develop an engaging offer for them to help achieve the library's ambition.

4

Understanding users and potential users

Now that you have considered library ambition within the strategic marketing process it is time to look at engaging with the people who will help the library to achieve that ambition. Marketing planners undertake significant market analysis before making choices of strategy. Textbooks sometimes refer to this as 'situation analysis' or 'environmental analysis'. Essentially, at this stage of marketing planning it is necessary to understand the marketplace within which the library service operates and the characteristics of that marketplace, which will open up or narrow the path to achieving engagement ambitions.

Most library services are competing in a number of different markets and it is appropriate to reflect on the markets served. For the purposes of marketing planning it is important to have quantified and qualitative measures of performance. Engagement activity is time and resource hungry and it is right that library managers should be confident of a good return for this investment.

In addition, to ensure that a library service has an appropriate, engaging offer in the marketplace, there is a need to create a deep understanding of what users and potential users value, require and want. Furthermore, how do they currently meet these needs and can we create a better offer than those of competitors? You should understand what gives competitors their place in the markets that libraries exist to serve.

Sources of funding for all types of library are increasingly uncertain and it is as important to engage with other stakeholders' values, needs, wants and priorities as it is to engage with those of users. Finally, you should track technological, social and other changes which will either support or constrain engagement with users and other stakeholders. Market research will provide an information base to help you with engaging offer development, communication and promotion.

Without a commitment to collecting, analysing and reporting data and information on library communities it is difficult to devise a realistic plan to meet clear objectives in the ambition as described in the previous chapter. This chapter outlines the key things a library manager must consider to ensure there is appropriate information input to the marketing plan. Any marketing strategy and plan must be based on knowledge of what is engaging to users and to research, which can be very complicated. Simply asking users 'what do you find engaging?' or 'what do you want from your library service?' is likely to be only part of the story that you need to create and tell.

Defining the marketplace

Defining the marketplace clearly is fundamental to effective marketing planning. It involves:

- *Measuring the library's share of users' and potential users' activity compared with competitors' shares.* If you do not have a clear picture of the library marketplace how will you be able to define the appropriate competitive landscape in which the library operates?
- *Understanding growth.* With a very loose definition of the marketplace it may be difficult to estimate growth rates. Defining a marketplace as education, information or recreation is mind boggling in its scope and not the basis for effective marketing planning; understanding the market as a series of sub-markets is much more useful. A 'boil the ocean' type strategy, in other words a potentially impossible set of activities to achieve given the reality of your resources, is almost certain to fail.
- *Identifying the groups of users or potential users who you wish to engage with.* If the library market is, in effect, defined as everything to everyone, it is difficult to identify key users or other stakeholders who will help you achieve your ambition. Without a clear focus your marketing planning process will result in over-generalised, non-engaging communications to users, potential users and other stakeholders. There will be a tendency to provide average offers to average users, who may or may not exist. For instance, public libraries are a universal service but this does not mean that there is one perfect public library service offering that fits all. The diversity of users' perceptions of value and their consequent needs and wants should be the basis for service decision and engagement programmes. This may involve prioritising activity by defining parts of the market that are to be served at the expense of others.
- *Recognising relevant competitors and what makes their services and products engaging to your users and potential users.* If you are not clear about what

market the library is competing in it is difficult to identify the relevant competitors to position library offers against. Why are competitors successful and are there any unmet market needs to be serviced?

■ *Developing marketing objectives and strategies.* Without a clear definition of the market how will you know what you can reasonably expect to achieve and what specific strategies will deliver the expected return?

■ *Creating and implementing clear marketing messages.* The defined market will provide the context to any messages developed. Without a clear definition of the markets served, the tone and language of the communication may not match that of those you wish to engage with.

Essentially your market definition provides a framework for your library activities and at this stage in the engagement process can simply be a statement of what products and services you will take to which legitimate user and potential user groups (Table 4.1).

Table 4.1 *Market definition of library activities*

My library service exists to take these products and services	
to these legitimate user and potential user groups	

Your reflection on these two parts of the sentence will provide the framework for library operations and engagement strategy. The definition may be amended as you progress through this book. Now you have a context in which to undertake your research into the markets you wish to engage with.

A marketing audit for engagement planning

It is likely that you already know much about your library service and the way users and potential users engage with it. After reflecting on what you already know you can close gaps in understanding by undertaking some degree of research. A marketing audit of users and potential users is appropriate using internal transactional information (issues, visits, enquiries, social media activity and other items) and external information (demographic and similar items). When looking at users' and potential users' relationship with the library (in a range from deeply engaged to totally unengaged or positively disengaged) it is always worthwhile studying what they actually engage with to see what has sparked their interest. Can the library use similar approaches or create similar experiences in other aspects of library service?

Library managers need this type of knowledge and understanding to align products and services into offers and value propositions (statements of why users should use you based on the value they seek and the value you provide) for individual groups within the library population or catchment area. When a clear information base about users and potential users is established, the competition the library faces, and our competitive competences and capabilities (everything from products and services to buildings, technological capabilities and staff), library managers can begin to plan either for traditional marketing strategies (marketing mix approaches – 6Ps: product, price, place, promotion, politics and partnerships – more Ps can be added as you will see later) or more personal customer relationship management approaches. It is not one or the other: library managers integrate both approaches into an engagement strategy.

The market audit should include a PESTLE analysis – an analysis of political, economic, social, technological, legal and environmental factors – to identify what may impact the library during the planning period (Table 4.2). A thorough review of the alternatives to libraries, in other words competitors, should also be undertaken. This wider analysis will provide context for offer development – the creation of an engaging offer for a group of users or potential users. It will be based on elements of the marketing mix above, together with a relationship strategy.

Are there implications for the library if the PESTLE analysis reveals areas where there will be significant changes in the library environment in coming years? Will the marketplace changes mean that users, potential users and stakeholders will be more or less likely to engage with the library in future? What changes will the library have to make if it is to remain important? Do the changes make the competitors weaker or stronger?

Table 4.2 *PESTLE analysis for library engagement*

	Changes expected during planning period	Implications for library service	Impact on competitors
Political			
Economic			
Social			
Technological			
Legal			
Environmental			

Understanding existing users

Chapter 9 looks at effective channels in which to advertise marketing strategy and prioritise potential future activity. To enable this prioritisation it is important, within your market definition, to understand the potential market that exists to be won and the actual market already captured by the library. In business this is often referred to as balancing customer acquisition and customer retention; in libraries this is best thought of as balancing user and potential user marketing.

Potential users as a category includes those who have never used a library before and those who have previously used the library but for some reason no longer do. The latter are lapsed users and a valuable source of information on how to stop engaged users disengaging. Did they cease using the library because the library did not deliver its promises, they no longer needed the library, or their requirements were satisfied elsewhere, or was it simply because the library offer was not engaging – it no longer inspired or enthused them?

Finding the right balance between allocating resources to engaged users and non-engaged users is fundamental to marketing planning. After all, it is inefficient to encourage use by new user groups if at the same time existing user groups are neglected, resulting in, figuratively, water draining out of the bottom of the bucket while trying to fill it from the top. Allowing some potential users to be disengaged while trying to engage others is not a very appealing strategy. It is a catechism of marketing that it takes between 5 and 15 times as much effort to win a new customer as it does to keep an existing customer, and a significant proportion of next year's activity will come from existing customers. Similarly in libraries the currently engaged are likely to be the mainstay of next year's visits, enquiries, issues or social media hits, likes or shares.

Any marketing planning process for libraries that balances these two strategies will only be effective if supported by excellent quality information and insight into what library users, potential users and other stakeholders might find engaging or unattractive in a library offer. Data-driven research is an increasingly important tool to help libraries achieve success because it is a source of information when drawing up marketing plans for engagement. Libraries have always collected data about their users and have used it to help plan services.

Data-driven market research

Data-driven market research can help address questions in a number of areas:

- *Research into key engagement issues.* What matters to users and potential users? What will draw them closer to the library? Where are they going in their lives and how can the library help them to achieve their goals?

■ *Descriptive research*. What are the important characteristics of the community the library serves? What is going on in users' lives? How do users access the service? When? How often? What works well for them? What does not? Why have some people never engaged at all with the library? Why have some people disengaged from the library?

■ *Predictive research*. What will happen if . . . [e.g., opening hours are changed]? What do library staff have to do to provide a more engaging offer than those of competitors?

■ *Feedback research*. How is the library doing? Are levels of satisfaction acceptable? Is the library service broadly on track or way off the pace in meeting users' expectations? Is the user experience improving or declining? Can we measure engagement with the library and its services?

From carrying out basic research in such areas the library manager can then move on to answer some of the deeper questions about creating and communicating appropriate and engaging messages. Very quickly the more interesting questions start to be raised, such as which groups use what library products and services, when, and why? What makes a collection of resources engaging? How should lifestyles be reflected in the library offer? Is our promotional and public relations activity engaging or simply one more message out there?

Research should be undertaken to answer a specific question not simply to find out more. Information can confuse as well as illuminate. Do not add to the information avalanche unless you know why you are collecting information and the specific decisions it will support at a particular time. Focus research on trying to find out what various library user and potential user groups find engaging. Is it presentation? Tone of language? The friendliness of staff? The library's sense of innovation? And so on.

Who are the real customers of a library service?

As managers in all marketplaces do, the librarian should disentangle the issue of customer and consumer. The person who uses the service may be the consumer but are they the customer? For example, in the public library arena, is the local politician the real customer as he or she, as a member of the local council, is the source of much of the funding public libraries receive? Or who is the customer of the children's library picture book collection? The child? Or the parent or guardian? For marketing this is an important question: the marketing messages must communicate with the real customer while not discouraging the consumer. If it is known who the real customers of a library service are when strategies are developed it is possible to create a powerful integrated mix of 'push' marketing communications (directed at intermediaries) and 'pull' marketing communications (directed at users or potential users). Engagement actions should be directed at the ultimate users and the influencers. A potential user may be inspired to use the library but at the same time be discouraged by an influencer with whom they are already deeply engaged.

An integrated marketing campaign for a children's picture book collection should be based on a detailed understanding of how issues, visits or funding are decided: messages to customers (parents), one message to consumers (children) and perhaps, where appropriate, messages to influencers (perhaps the school staff). This 'decision-making unit' should not be overlooked. Messages to only one part of this unit lose the potential to benefit from the cumulative power of integrated messaging even if they initially have an impact. Much more effective is a managed campaign to engage all involved in any decisions made. An understanding of the various decision-making units that have an impact on library service should be part of any marketing planning audit, looking at users and potential users. In Chapter 6 we introduce other stakeholders.

Take some time to reflect on what you know about your user or potential user groups and complete Table 4.3.

Table 4.3 *Influences of decision-making units on library use*

Library product, service or offer	Customers (major decision-makers on use)	Consumers (people who actually use the library)	Influencers (people who influence use of the library)

Table 4.3 provides a template of the groups of people to address in messages as part of an integrated marketing engagement campaign when marketing a specific product, service or offer. Try to create engaging messages to all, reflecting the different approaches they may take or respond to. For advice on how to formulate and integrate these messages see Chapter 8.

Understanding and engaging potential users

As noted earlier, there are two distinct types of potential users to research and understand:

- users who have never engaged with the library
- users who used to be users of the library but, for whatever reason, have disengaged from the library (lapsed users).

It is harder to research and understand potential users than users. By their very nature non-users are less likely to be interested in contributing towards your knowledge of their lives and potential library activities. However, lapsed users may be very vocal in contributing information, especially if they have disengaged because of a bad experience with the library. They are likely to be excellent sources of actionable information provided that the library has a commitment to change. If your glass is half empty then a complaint is a failure. If your glass is half full then a complaint is an opportunity to improve and a very valuable source of information for marketing planning. Never be put off researching lapsed users for fear of unleashing complaints. There can be perfectly good reasons for lapsed use – changes of circumstances, life stage or lifestyle. Each one has important marketing implications for offer development or marketing communications and is a key item of marketing information.

Many libraries have undertaken non-user surveys and there is a good body of knowledge as to why people don't visit libraries, for example:

- *Lifestyle*. Many people do not find that library services fit in with the way in which they live their lives. To engage with these folks may involve increasing online and remote services rather than trying to draw them to a physical space.
- *Resources and stock*. Some potential library users do not use the library because they do not believe that the library has the type of stock they would find useful and attractive. This may be true but also may simply be the result of there being ineffective communication between users and library staff about stock range and availability.
- *Ambience*. For some groups the library is an unattractive environment, not a 'cool' place to be. The rules and culture discourage some potential users.
- *Access*. Some potential users find it difficult to access libraries, despite significant commitment by libraries to digital offerings. They may be disabled, live in rural areas, have to rely on very poor public transport links, or have limited knowledge of the home country's language.
- *Customer service*. It is not always easy to recover a user who has disengaged after a bad experience when using the library, and such users are likely to tell all who will listen just how bad it was.

These are some reasons potential users have given in surveys asking why they don't use a library: 'I get my information elsewhere', 'I'm not interested', 'I'm too busy and have other interests', 'I buy my own books', 'There is a lack of choice' or 'I have no need of the library'. Clearly there is scope for new marketing strategies to educate and persuade, but at this market audit stage attempt to understand exactly why potential users have given these reasons. If users are 'too busy' to use the library should we address the fact that the way we deliver service is not convenient and fast enough? The answers to such questions have real impact on the way we develop and deliver effective, engaging library services. For marketing purposes information must not just be collected but be understood. Librarians need to know what readers say on comments forms and in surveys, and what they mean by what they say.

Good quality research is undertaken to answer specific questions rather than to simply 'find out more'. A good discipline at the outset of a research project is to try to formulate proposed outcomes and actions for each question, for example, 'If over 75% of people answer B to question 3 then we will . . .'. While this cannot be done for every question in a market research survey, this exercise focuses attention on actionable information. If you cannot formulate such statements for the potential answers to any of the questions in the survey you may find it difficult to come to any conclusions at the analysis stage of the survey.

Collecting information

Having decided what information is required, how should it be collected? Before rushing straight to a survey, librarians should ask themselves what decisions this survey will influence. Once library managers are clear about how information supports decision-making processes they can choose the most appropriate tool or technique to discover the required information. Here are a few thoughts to consider before undertaking a survey:

- It is not always helpful in a survey to ask users what they really want. If people are simply asked what they want they will tend to want everything and for free, or will assume that what they want is going to be too expensive for the library and thus do not even mention it.
- In other instances users or potential users do not know what they want, make up a 'wish list', and then do not use new services you implement as a result.
- With non-user surveys, choose sample size and frame carefully to avoid legitimate criticisms of representativeness. You may need to carry out 'snowball' sampling to achieve some degree of rigour. Snowball sampling simply entails asking the few people you know who are representative of the group you are surveying if they know others like themselves. Then sample these people as well. This can be a particularly appropriate approach for hard to reach groups who are very rarely, if ever, exposed to library service at the moment.

- Sometimes experiments are more useful and timely than research.
- Surveys can lead to a policy of continuous improvement rather than innovation – continuous improvement, while potentially relevant for developing services for existing users, may not be enough to attract potential users or lapsed users.

Creating an information base

These are some specific tools and techniques to use to create an information base: desk research, focus groups, survey research, observation and ethnography. Data can be primary data (created specifically for a survey) or secondary data (created for other purposes but useful in your specific library study).

The choice of technique depends on whether the issues being researched require quantitative data (numerical or quantified data) or qualitative data (non-numerical or unquantified data). It is perfectly acceptable to collect both as part of the same research exercise.

If it is necessary to count characteristics, for example to estimate potential levels of use for library services, then the research should generate quantitative data; if the requirement is to understand user engagement, perceptions, motivations, lifestyles, needs and wants, for example to develop clear library offers, then research output is driven by qualitative data.

Here are some library examples of these types of data:

- *Quantitative data*, for example age, gender, ethnicity. Regardless of what they think and believe, users and potential users possess these 'hard' characteristics. They may not be the main determinants of why and how individuals access libraries but they are classifications.
- *Qualitative data*, such as experience of using online resources, expectations of library layout, reactions to a new library, satisfaction with service provision. This type of 'soft' data is based on user expectations, feelings and perceptions so it is essentially qualitative in nature and key to understanding actual or potential levels of engagement that you can expect.

Modern strategic marketing managers are especially interested in qualitative data when deciding the range of products and services they should create and develop, and are interested in quantitative data to measure potential levels of use and performance – market share and penetration. Library managers should likewise recognise the benefits of using both types of data in library engagement planning. The quantified information is important to give evidence of performance and the qualitative information provides a powerful basis for developing engaging offers and subsequent marketing communications. Put more simply, quantitative data is useful to engage funding stakeholders in understanding how well the library is doing; qualitative information is particularly useful in engaging users and potential users, encouraging them to come through the door, to visit the website or to contact the library via telephone, e-mail or social media.

What information do we already have?

Here are some examples of the types of secondary desk research that libraries may be able to collate without commissioning new field research:

- *Previous library surveys.* Although care must be taken when using past library surveys, they can be a useful starting point when carrying out new research. The most useful previous library surveys are those that have been undertaken regularly, because they provide time series data enabling an understanding of changes in user activities or perceptions of service. One-off snapshot surveys, often on specific topics, have some relevance but unless undertaken very recently are compromised and not likely to gain the confidence of library planners.
- *Suggestion and complaint files.* Most libraries take complaints and suggestions very seriously and may have files of them. Although care must be taken to avoid distorting the perception of the whole library service because of one or two disengaged and vociferous users, such complaints may represent a view not always raised by the majority of the potential user group so should not be automatically dismissed.
- *Articles in the academic and professional literature.* It is surprising how much is already known about the way that libraries operate in their communities. Remember that reinventing the wheel is time-consuming, expensive and pointless.

When searching for desk research data it is worthwhile asking who is likely to need that data to be able to do their job. A quick telephone call to the appropriate person can often save many hours of research in the library. Secondary desk research data is likely to be readily available and may not be especially expensive. The limitation of desk research is that since the data was gathered by other people for other purposes, it may not be totally appropriate to the current problem the library is addressing because of methodology or assumptions that were used in its creation. For example, library surveys, even if undertaken every year, may well reflect current and past uses rather than provide true insight into the future needs of users and un-served users. One valuable use of secondary desk research is in the compilation of a community profile.

Profiling your potential library community

As noted earlier, good marketing of library services is based on a sound information base. Clearly, if engaging offers and messages are to be created, a library manager needs to know as much about users and potential users as possible. A profile provides basic building blocks of a marketing approach to library services and contains simple information about the population to be served, which can be used as a very powerful input to user segmentation (see Chapter 5). Community profiles have been particularly popular with public library authorities at various times but are relevant to all types of library.

What is a profile of the community and why produce one?

A community profile is a detailed description of a group of people who think of themselves as a community and is in many cases created with their co-operation. A community can be students within an academic institution, members of the public within a local authority area, the full range of clinical professional and administrative staff within a health authority, or even the range of departments, project teams and influencers within a corporate library.

Many public libraries already have a community profiling exercise underway to help evaluate the introduction of various central and local government initiatives. While these will often be simply quantifications of various population characteristics, they can provide a baseline for the type of community profiling especially useful for developing segmentation. Furthermore, this mapping of the user and potential user population can help staff evaluate the success or otherwise of subsequent marketing communication activities.

Finally, undertaking a community profiling exercise can have a subtle marketing impact. Marketing is increasingly seen as developing engagement rather than simply sending out messages. For example, in a public library authority, if a library has a community profile a librarian has a genuine reason to contact local groups and organisations, which helps build trust between the community and the library service, and the community profile can demonstrate the library's commitment to developing services around a full understanding of the community. However, if this appears to be little more than a 'tick box' exercise, more harm than good will be done to your engagement and marketing activities. Should the discussions during your profiling exercise identify significant library shortcomings, the library community may reasonably expect you to do something to address them. Failure to respond does not create a good atmosphere for engagement.

Communities of interest or communities of need?

As noted above, many community profiles, particularly in public libraries, are based around local government administrative areas and defined by the type of library context. Within an academic library, for instance, the community might be the whole body of students, and academic, administrative and operational staff.

From a marketing point of view, there is support for the idea of including specific sub-profiles within the exercise (for instance lesbian, gay, bisexual and transgender communities, refugees and specific ethnic communities in public libraries) or communities of need (for example project teams in corporate libraries, or clinicians in health service libraries). These profiles of communities of interest or communities of need can be organisation-wide and help ensure that important user segments are not lost within wider service planning.

What should go into the community profile?

There are many things you may need to know about your user and potential user population. For example, the community profile of a public library would include:

- *socio-economic information*, as social classifications and employment patterns can be helpful when targeting services
- *demographic information*, as knowing age structures can help when creating the right atmospheres in libraries and ensure that marketing communications have the right tone of voice
- *information on social deprivation*, as the mission of public libraries often includes improving the quality of life of individuals – a thorough understanding of social deprivation and what it means in practice for people can be a very useful part of the community profile
- *housing, health and educational characteristics*, which add useful planning detail and may resonate with current library authority priorities.

Often public libraries cease their community profiling activities when they have collected this sort of quantitative information. However, there is an opportunity to add a degree of sophistication by supplementing quantitative information with qualitative information, for example on:

- *lifestyles*, how people live their lives, what the social patterns are
- *life stages*, such as having a family and retiring, as these should be reflected in the way public library services are delivered
- *hopes*, what the community hopes to achieve
- *fears*, what constrains the community in achieving its goals, so services can be developed to address them
- *attitudes*, as users' beliefs, expectations, opinions, perceptions and feelings about life and community should be considered when planning a library service.

Academic library community profiles, too, can mix quantitative and qualitative data. Qualitative data, for example on the student life cycle and mental health concerns, can present as much opportunity for engagement as a mere analysis of quantitative data. These are examples of qualitative data:

- *relationships to university* (student, faculty, administrative, external businesses and others)
- *course choices* (faculties, undergraduate, postgraduate taught, postgraduate research)
- *types of resources accessed* (full range, mainly online, or mainly in library)
- *types of special needs* (access requirements, study skills abilities).

A simple community profile consisting entirely of quantitative data tends to stereotype users and potential users because people cannot be defined solely by a single characteristic. People are complex and not always consistent. They often operate and act in different ways in different contexts.

How to obtain data for the community profile

When you have decided on the outline for your community profile and are seeking data, first find out if anyone has collected most or any of this information already. Community profiling is undertaken by a wide variety of organisations and it is always worthwhile undertaking an initial sweep for previous projects, especially if your engagement planning is for public libraries. Data may be out of date, but even so will act as a good guide to the sources of information you can use. You may find data from local and national government departments, academic institutions, religious groups, health authorities, police authorities, community associations and newspapers.

Once you have collected as much data as possible from these sources, you will have to undertake some of your own research. The quantitative data will be relatively easy to find, if time-consuming. It is significantly harder to acquire qualitative data and will almost certainly involve you in undertaking focus groups and wider user and potential user depth surveys. Do not underestimate the amount of time and expertise required to undertake such activities.

When completed, a community profile is a useful resource as it helps you to:

- *plan services*: estimate the engagement opportunity for current or proposed services and begin the process of market segmentation
- *evaluate services*: understand the relative proportions of particular or potential user groups so it is possible to evaluate your effectiveness in serving them and inspire library use
- *identify resources in a community*: by undertaking a community profile encourage library managers to identify information resources on, and within, their community
- *develop links with organisations and communities*: as part of the search for information build valuable links with potentially useful organisations
- *support funding bids*: as partnerships and new sources of funding are key drivers in library management throughout the world, use a community profile as evidence when bidding for funds.

Survey research

If you want to quantify data about any aspect of engagement planning which is not revealed by desk research, it may be appropriate to carry out a survey. When there is a representative sample of users, it is possible to estimate take-up or deeper engagement for particular services or users' general views on a simple issue. However, beware. These are always simply estimations, because no survey can fully consider all the factors that influence how people use a library service.

Surveys are time-consuming for library staff to undertake and for those surveyed to complete. Do not rush too quickly to a survey when you may be able to make reasonable estimates about a particular matter from your desk research data. However, if the information you already have about users is either out of date or does not help with future decision-making, you may decide to invest time and other resources to generate more information through a survey.

How to undertake a survey

If you decide that a survey is the best way to collect information you require, be very clear exactly what you need to research and identify research objectives (what you want the survey to reveal). If possible, be clear not only what areas the survey should shed light upon but also have a view on how you will be able to interpret the results. Hold your nerve with agreed simple research objectives and if you find yourself saying 'it would be nice to know . . .' or 'while we're asking this we might as well ask . . .', challenge yourself on how you will use the information you hope to obtain. As libraries in all sectors always seek to get value for money there will be a natural tendency to look for a seemingly best value approach to user research. More does not necessarily mean better or more actionable research.

Check that what you need to know is not already known

Many non-user surveys have now been undertaken around the world so there is a clear body of information on the reasons for non-use of a library. Non-user surveys undertaken without reviewing previous work are likely to provide very similar research without adding new dimensions for marketing planning. Remember your research activity is to support your planning process not to provide an academically rigorous information base. That is the remit of others and there is no need to replicate this when their findings are publicly available.

Devise a research proposal and brief

Consider whether to undertake your research project in-house or instruct an outside agency to complete it. Market research is always a project so should be rigorously project managed with a lead project manager to take responsibility for delivering the project's objectives within timescale and budget.

These are the main advantages of undertaking the process internally:

■ You understand what you are researching.
■ You do not have a long learning curve before you can begin productive work.
■ You have an opportunity to develop engagement.

These are the main disadvantages of undertaking the process internally:

■ You may bias the project because of your knowledge.

- You may not implement, complete and analyse the process because you have limited staff resources or another initiative takes precedence.

These are the main advantages of asking an external agency to carry out the research:

- There is an agreed deadline to which the agency will deliver.
- The agency staff should be expert in carrying out a survey.
- The sole basis of the agency's relationship with the library is to deliver in full on time. Provided that the library delivers its part of the research process in allocating time for meetings and other agreed activities there can be few reasons for non-completion within an agreed timescale.

Whatever approach is agreed the research brief and proposal should include a plan with an estimate of time and other costs.

Choose a research method

If an outside agency is used the staff will be able to advise on appropriate ways to ask questions and analyse responses. Quantitative data collection methods include in-library self-completion questionnaires, telephone surveys and e-mail surveys. Traditionally postal surveys have been a research option but modern lifestyles suggest that there are very few, if any, instances where they would be appropriate in current library contexts. Qualitative methods include focus groups, depth interviews, experiments and other ethnographic approaches.

E-mail surveys can be useful if the group to be surveyed is likely to be a heavy user of such communications channels. In some library contexts there may be a very poor response rate to surveys, however. For instance, students nowadays rarely use e-mail as a major source of communication and it may be difficult to engage their interest to complete an e-mail survey. You may need to offer some inducement (e.g. free printing credits or the promise of a contribution to charity for each completed survey). You could e-mail people directing respondents to a hidden section of the library website where a questionnaire can be completed, or leave an open questionnaire on the institution's website. However, this may only attract people who like filling in questionnaires and is hardly a robust method of data collection.

Identify the sample

As librarians are rarely able to undertake a census of the population (talk to every legitimate or potential user of the library service), a sample has to suffice. Who are you going to talk to? Some libraries undertake service-wide surveys based on self-selecting, self-completion questionnaires picked up from library desks. Take care using such an approach with questionnaires as they will be completed almost exclusively by users who like filling them in. You need to monitor and control who completes the questionnaires to ensure that sufficient numbers of each category of users of interest are included in the final collection of completed forms. A slightly more rigorous approach is to instruct staff to hand out forms to every sixth or tenth member of the public at particular times of day. This gives the illusion of random sampling.

One of the first questions to consider is how many people to sample. A simple answer in many organisational contexts is 'as many as we can afford to sample'. If statistical significance is required, use a formula for calculating appropriate sample size.

There are two key concepts to consider when identifying a statistically significant sample size – the confidence interval and the confidence level:

- The *confidence interval* is the plus or minus figure usually reported in opinion poll results in the media. For example, if you use a confidence interval of 4 (3% or 4% is probably a reasonable interval for most library surveys) and 40% of your sample picks an answer, you can be confident that if you had asked the question of the entire relevant population then between 36% (40–4) and 44% (40+4) would have picked that answer.
- The *confidence level* tells you how sure you can be. It is expressed as a percentage and represents how often the true percentage of the population who would pick an answer lies within the confidence interval. A 95% confidence level means you can be 95% certain; a 99% confidence level means you can be 99% certain. It is usual to accept a 95% confidence level.

In the example above, if you combine the confidence level and the confidence interval together you can say that you are 95% sure that the true percentage of the population is between 36% and 44%. If the population you are surveying consists of 1,000 individuals then you would need a sample size of 375 individuals.

Sample size calculators are freely available on the internet so thankfully you do not need to undertake complex calculations yourself. Many market research companies mount calculators on their websites as a free service where you simply need to put in the number of people in the population you are studying together with the degree of confidence you seek (usually 95% confidence level and 3 or 4 as an acceptable interval). Type 'sample size calculator' into your favourite search engine and you will have a selection to browse through.

Sampling for potential user surveys can be a difficult problem as you will often not be able to identify where all the members of a particular group can be contacted. In such cases snowball sampling is appropriate. In its simplest formulation this consists of identifying respondents who are then used to refer researchers on to other respondents. Snowball sampling contradicts many of the assumptions underpinning rigorous sampling but has advantages for sampling populations such as the socially stigmatised and newly emerging lifestyle segments.

Pilot your survey

Before running the survey, pilot whatever survey instrument you plan to use to ensure that it will work in practice in a similar way to the way you thought it would when devising it. You are likely at this stage to find you need to make at least some small changes to any intended questionnaire or other survey instrument. When confident that the survey will uncover understandable and usable data, you can move on to run the research project in earnest.

Revise the survey instrument

Revising a survey instrument (often a questionnaire) following the pilot should not be seen as failure of the draft. Ideally you will make positive amendments that improve the quality of the survey instrument.

Run survey and collect data

If you have instructed a market research agency to undertake the survey the agency staff will manage the project, but you will be responsible for attending meetings and providing information agreed at the beginning of the project. It is always wise to contact the agency occasionally to check how things are going. If undertaking this project in-house ensure that it is managed efficiently. There are numerous books that offer help on running a market research survey and collecting data.

Analyse data

Analysis of data takes place in the context of the original research problem that prompted the project. There are a number of very useful market research software products available that enable market research data to be analysed efficiently. These include products from companies such as SurveyMonkey and SmartSurvey which let you carry out basic surveys for free but others attract a fee. As noted above, if a market research agency has been commissioned its staff will have expertise to undertake the survey and ensure robust results. One advantage of online surveys is that you can often access real-time analysis of responses to date, which can provide early warning of possible results at the end of the project. However, you should not jump to conclusions too quickly as rigorous and valid results will only be possible when the appropriate total number of respondents has been collected.

Present research results

It is now usual for market research agencies to present research results as a PowerPoint presentation supplemented by data tables rather than compile a full document report. Keep in mind who will receive the research results and what they intend to do with them. Some audiences like to see a detailed methodology with sample size breakdowns; others prefer top-level summaries with action points clearly derived from the data.

Collect qualitative information for engagement planning

Qualitative data is best collected through focus groups, surveys and ethnographic methods. They can go beyond quantification to investigating the information needs of certain user groups by looking at their lifestyles and life events, recreational interests, educational desires and preferred ways to access services.

Although focus groups and surveys are the most widely used ways to generate such information there are ethnographic methods too, such as observation and undertaking experiments, which in particular circumstances are more appropriate than speaking to users directly. For example, looking at user behaviour in libraries is an ideal observational technique, as users often forget the details of everything they have done on a library visit; or a potential new service may be so beyond the current experience of library users that it may be appropriate to undertake an experiment to understand users' reactions and behaviour rather than ask them what they think of the potential new service.

Focus groups

A focus group is a structured group interview with participants who are members of the target user group. In essence it is an opportunity for the library to listen to users or potential users and for users to discuss their views, perceptions, expectations and feelings about libraries. It is unusual to undertake a single focus group, indeed you may need to undertake a number of them to feel confident that you have heard the diversity of views and discussion of the group you are studying.

Focus groups are useful to identify the key questions to include in a library survey on a particular topic and to test the likely responses to new initiatives or changes in library service. They can thus be used either early or late in the research process but are not a standalone exercise. A focus group reveals consensus and diversity of opinion.

Focus groups are not appropriate if you intend to count things as part of your research. They always comprise a non-random sample from a target segment of users whose views cannot on their own be used to justify changing a service in a particular way.

There are several stages to conducting a focus group, which are discussed below.

Appoint a project manager

Appoint a project manager immediately the decision has been made to undertake focus groups.

Identify an experienced moderator

The role of the moderator (sometimes called facilitator) is to run the focus group and report back on the proceedings. The moderator should be skilled in managing group interactions. While it is possible to use an existing member of library staff to undertake this role, do not underestimate the value of asking a trained professional to tease out important information. An ideal moderator has an outgoing personality and can bring out all points of view from all attendees, some of whom may be more reticent than others. The moderator (whether a member of library staff or an independent professional) should encourage open discussion and avoid asking leading questions. Library staff should be heavily involved in setting up the topic guide for the focus group and fully brief any external moderator on the meaning of all key concepts as required.

The project manager should co-ordinate the key ideas, questions or issues to be put before the focus group attendees and agree the topic guide in conjunction with the moderator. Here are some example areas where a focus group would provide especially useful data, insights and opinions:

- to react to potential new services
- to react to recently introduced new services

- to ask views on library guiding
- to give thoughts about using the library
- to describe feelings about visiting the library
- to clarify results of surveys.

Focus groups are especially valuable when trying to find out how people feel about the library and its services or where their opinions are important, such as in the early stages of designing a new modern library building, or where library staff have to decide which is the better of two alternative actions, and finding out what the reaction is to them is potentially useful before making a final decision. Focus groups can be built around possible futures or used to find out how services have been received by the user group.

Be sure that your focus group does indeed have focus. These groups should not be used simply to provide a general talking shop or to quantify what can easily be researched from secondary sources. You should have a clear idea about how the data, once collected, will be analysed. Keep this in mind when developing the guide topics or questions for the group.

Identify and book an appropriate venue

The venue for holding the focus group should have appropriate facilities and atmosphere. It is usually appropriate to speak to library users in a comfortable area with soft furnishings. Armchairs and sofas facilitate a relaxed discussion within the group. However, some target segments may benefit from a focus group being held in a hard area with a boardroom table and chairs to facilitate a formal discussion, for example if you were undertaking a focus group with business people to consider developments in the business information service in a corporate library. Then members of the group may feel comfortable discussing topics of concern when sitting around a boardroom-style table.

It is appropriate to use the library as a venue, provided there is an area which can offer the right atmosphere and it is likely that potential attendees would be willing to visit the library. Some people, particularly non-users, may be more prepared to join a focus group if it is held outside the library. You may be tempted to try to get these non-users into the library, arguing that you wish to expose them to its services, but beware: the whole purpose of a focus group is to gather information to help understand the issue being studied, not to promote the service. Promote the service on another occasion. It is not good practice to have too many objectives for a focus group, and never forget their primary purpose.

Identify and invite potential focus group members

Focus groups work best with six to twelve participants in order to encourage discussion. It is advisable to aim to attract at least ten group members as often unforeseen circumstances lead to one or more being unable to attend a meeting. A focus group of fewer than six participants is unlikely to be productive.

When considering who to invite to join a focus group be aware that you are not attempting to reflect the whole community in one focus group. To deliver useful information, it is important that the group is not made up of a mix of library users who are likely to have highly conflicting views. For example, a focus group to consider future services within a health service library will not be productive if it consists of two surgeons, two GPs, two administrators, two nurses and two from professions allied to health. It would be much more appropriate to run individual focus groups for each of these categories of stakeholder. In a large library you may need to conduct in excess of ten focus groups. It is extremely unlikely that one will be enough for any project.

It is also unlikely that a focus group would benefit from having users and potential users in the same focus group. The difference in experience and knowledge of the library would be too great to encourage meaningful discussion. Be wary if you use posters seeking recruits to a focus group that you do not attract people who only apply to join the group because they enjoy attending focus group meetings.

Contact attendees by letter, phone, e-mail, text or WhatsApp reminding them about the meeting about a week before it is held. Explain the importance of them being present in order to give their views, and ask them to confirm they will attend. Consider rewarding attendance by donating to charity, or giving participants retail vouchers or cash. There are opportunities to tailor the reward for particular groups. For instance, a group of public library fiction readers might be rewarded by being allowed an agreed number of free book reservations; students in an academic library could be rewarded by being given printing credits.

Conduct the focus group

Welcome participants as they arrive and do not forget to offer refreshments, which should relax them. Keep the atmosphere relaxed but professional. Ensure participants know the purpose of the meeting, in what way participants are similar, and the process that the focus group will follow. It is usual for meetings to last between 60 and 90 minutes.

The value of focus groups is to elicit a range of views on the issue under discussion. Group discussion helps individuals develop their views and is known to encourage better recall of ideas and insight. One of the tasks of the moderator is to draw comment from the diffident and manage the outspoken.

Consider recording the meeting, though if you wish to do so make sure to obtain permission from the attendees. It is acceptable to use flip charts to note salient points as the meeting progresses. As audio and video equipment can suffer from malfunctions such as flat batteries or human error in operation it is always wise to ensure someone takes notes of what is said.

Produce a report

Produce a report of the focus group together with an analysis of the key topics that form the bases for the structure of the focus group meeting. This need not be more than a series of bullet points, but liberal uses of (non-attributed) actual quotes from attendees is often valuable. The specific words and phrases used can be very revealing and provide the vocabulary for any subsequent surveys. Consider sharing this report with attendees. At the very least, your attendees should be offered a summary of the proceedings.

Researching user experience and satisfaction

Engagement with a library service develops from a person's experience of using that library service, exposure to its marketing and publicity activities and, to some extent, the opinions and experiences of trusted friends and colleagues. Traditional library surveys and focus groups can provide some understanding in this area, but for deep understanding of user experience, design-thinking-led ethnographic methods need to be employed.

Much of traditional research into library user needs has mainly taken account of what people say about the existing service or potential future service. Reflection on what users actually do is often as revealing for future library service development as what users say.

This shift from looking at 'what they say' to looking at 'what they do' is at the heart of ethnographic approaches to collecting useful data about users and their deep needs from library service. While this approach works best with existing users it can be used to help understand the activities and habits of potential users too, if they are studied in appropriate environments. For example, studying the general online behaviour of particular user groups may give hints as to how a library's digital presence should be structured and how the user journey through the online environment unfolds.

Ethnographers gather information using a variety of qualitative and quantitative sources and techniques. At their most sophisticated, researchers become participant observers. Their deep immersion in how people act and their hopes, fears, behaviour and attitudes gives them a fuller picture of a group of users or potential users than that derived from studying the results of one type of data collection. In addition to carrying out surveys and focus groups, ethnographers may observe and take field notes, analyse documents, keep photo journals, create stories, undertake unobtrusive testing, 'mystery shopping' and process mapping, and write diaries. Ethnographic research can be an important technique within a 'design thinking' approach or in more general user experience projects. At the very least it can remove the distance between the researcher and library users, allowing the possibility of deep understanding. Traditionally lone researchers have undertaken ethnographic research but in recent years a team approach has become evident, allowing more reflection and deeper analysis.

To take one example of this ethnographic approach, managers at the University of Illinois in Chicago asked staff on the reference desk to consider 'what are we doing?', 'what are the students doing?', 'what are we doing for the students?' and 'how could we do it better?'. Reflection on these questions led to changes in orientation requirements, instruction requirements and the curriculum. While academic libraries have been the most conspicuous converts to ethnographic research it is not a sector specific technique. All library managers could benefit from adopting these tools, provided they recognise that this technique requires significant commitment if true insights are to be generated.

Satisfied customers of a service are likely to tell a few of their friends of their experience, but dissatisfied customers are likely to tell even more people. Those managing any modern library marketing or engagement strategy will recognise the importance of user retention, which involves keeping users satisfied. A user's satisfaction will not be sufficient for that person to develop engagement and stay loyal to any particular service, especially if there is competition from other providers, but it is certainly necessary to keep them on board. Think back to your experiences of shopping, and times when you have been satisfied with a product, but still bought a different one next time simply because you wanted a change. However, if you had been dissatisfied you would certainly have bought another item instead, unless there was no substitute for it. Given this importance it is therefore essential that user satisfaction is monitored and any drop in standards addressed urgently.

Understanding competition

Once you are convinced that you understand the needs and wants of users and potential users and, most importantly, that the offer you have is delivered satisfactorily, it is always worth looking at other options a user or potential user may have in meeting those needs and wants. A moment's reflection will highlight that most libraries have competition for what they offer, for example, a search engine on a desk in a corporate environment, or a bargain books box in a charity shop for someone looking for a quick read.

Be sure to study competitive offers which your users and potential users receive as it can help you decide what your offer, or value proposition, should be. In other words, what value do you offer to your library community that will encourage individuals to engage with you in preference to other alternatives on offer?

Value is defined by users, and is discussed in Chapter 5. What a librarian perceives as value in library service may or may not be the same as what library users and potential users perceive to be of value in library service. Whether users engage with your offer or that of a competitor depends on the relative value to the user of using you rather than one of the alternatives.

When considering users' requirements be honest about whether your library service provides the best way to satisfy them. If it does not, then your marketing communications must be especially persuasive and it is possible that you need to enhance your value proposition and offer.

Who are your competitors and why? How can you make a superior offer in the marketplace? This is key information you need for your marketing planning. Complete Table 4.4 to ensure you have sufficient knowledge to underpin your thinking in later chapters of this book.

When reflecting on what you have included in Table 4.4 keep in mind the

Table 4.4 *Calculating the competition for the attention of users for individual library products, services or offers*

Library product, service, offer or user group	Competitor	Competitor's strengths and weaknesses	Our relative position compared with competitors (superior, equal, inferior)

fundamental question – 'how do we ensure that we have the winning offer?'.
These are some examples of competitors:

- *in corporate libraries*: colleagues, external information brokers, search engines
- *in public libraries*: bookshops, charity shops, search engines

■ *in academic libraries*: Google Scholar, other search engines
■ *in health libraries*: colleagues, friends, national libraries.

Identifying competitors and completing Table 4.4 will help you to understand why you do particularly well or badly in certain areas of service or product. Your list of competitors can include 'do nothing' and any other use of time. Formulate competitors' strengths and weaknesses by considering how users or potential users would talk about them, and look for strengths and weaknesses in the way they deliver specific products or services, not simply their general organisation-wide strengths and weaknesses.

Figure 4.1 shows another way of presenting similar information to emphasise the relative importance to users of valuable elements within an offer. The key qualities the user group is looking for (knowledgeable staff, speed, etc.) are identified and plotted according to their relative importance. Once the list is completed showing the relative importance of each element, the performance of alternative sources of supply (competitors) are similarly plotted.

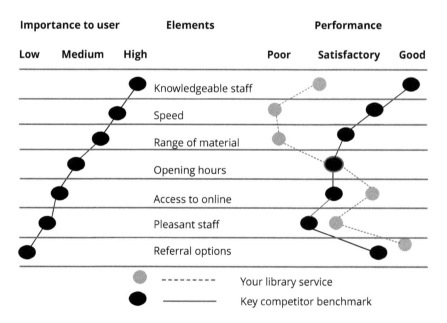

Figure 4.1 *Example of competitive benchmarking*

This analysis can only be undertaken at user group or segment level, it does not make sense to plot this type of information for the library service as a whole. For instance, having 'access to online' may be very important to some public library groups (e.g. teenagers) but relatively less so for other groups such as the general recreational fiction user. Although having 'access to online' may still be relevant for the latter group it is not a key factor in what drives them to use the library. These nuances need to be researched as part of the market analysis. Each factor is either relatively more or less important to specific groups and averaging out importance does not reflect the requirements of different user groups when offers are being created.

In the notional example of competitive benchmarking shown in Figure 4.1 the library and its key benchmark appear at first sight to have similar strengths in specific aspects of service required by the user or user group. Indeed, without considering the relative importance of each factor it would be tempting to say that the library and its competitor are roughly equal in strength, as each is superior in three characteristics, and in one characteristic they are of equal strength. However, on reflection, the library is in a very vulnerable position. Even though it has superior access to online, pleasant staff and referral options, these are less important to the user or user group than knowledgeable staff, speed of response and range of material, in each of which the library is significantly outperformed by the key benchmark. The marketing planning implications here are clear – consider improving the offer before undertaking marketing communications. Although users are unlikely to have perfect knowledge of the options available to them there is the opportunity to increase the chance of successful marketing and engagement.

Competition need not always be necessary or undesirable. Where different organisations have similar goals, collaboration and partnerships are possible and are to be encouraged. At the market audit stage you should understand needs and competitive offers thoroughly to identify opportunities for collaboration and engagement.

By now your head may well be spinning with the range of tools and techniques available to you to carry out market planning or an engagement project. There are many more. Analysing the results of desk research, surveys, focus groups, user experience studies, unobtrusive testing and competitor studies within a situational analysis of the environment the library operates in will give rich data to underpin planning for engagement.

Market analysis highlights diversity and differences rather than neat and tidy classification in what a library service should offer. Users and potential users exhibit a wide range of characteristics and the competitive landscape is complicated by competitors targeting specific groups of users and potential users.

Your level of engagement with chosen user groups will to a great extent be underpinned by your degree of knowledge and understanding of those you wish to engage with. The next chapter considers how you can segment by value sought to reflect the needs of diverse user groups and help you develop engaging offers.

5

Identifying value and segmentation

To encourage deep user and stakeholder engagement a library service must have something of value to offer to users, potential users and stakeholders. Furthermore it needs to be able to communicate and deliver that value in an attractive, consistent and reliable way.

But what is value? Value is anything that helps users or stakeholders get to where they want to go in an environment full of noisy, often irrelevant, messages. Everyone attempts to engage with services that will speed them to their chosen destination efficiently, effectively and enjoyably, with as little hassle and as inexpensively as possible. The destination may be a career aspiration, a lifestyle choice, a simple ongoing task or even a nice warm feeling of contentment.

Not all sources of value are equal and for the librarian's desire to engage to align with the user's willingness to engage the most important sources of value need to be provided by the library as uniquely as possible. There is value in scarcity and significantly less value if the source of value is easily accessed across a whole range of competitive suppliers. The analysis of competition at the end of Chapter 4 will have provided you with an understanding of how unique your value is likely to be.

General features and benefits of library service are not necessarily valuable to readers, even if librarians think they are. They only become valuable if individuals find them so. For the service you provide to be truly engaging you must have a deep understanding of your users rather than simply give them what fellow professionals think is important.

Value, as noted above, is ultimately defined by library users and other stakeholder groups rather than by the library service. Library staff may have some views on what is valuable but beware of simply assuming that what you think is valuable about libraries will be shared by non-librarians. The outputs from the activities suggested in Chapter 4 should have highlighted some areas of potential value and inspired early ideas about how to create winning and engaging offers and messages. However, it is likely that you will have noticed that not all potential users and stakeholders are looking for the same values, so before creating offers and messages, users and stakeholders need to be grouped to focus on this development.

In the absence of this degree of understanding librarians might simply define what the library is good at, or wishes to be seen as, and get the message out. Remember though that trying to get engagement with some part of service that is not included as part of the natural value for the user is not likely to be successful. Marketing professionals are often accused of trying to get people to want what they did not really want, but every experienced marketer emphasises that this is not the main thrust of effective marketing.

Each user and stakeholder group may have different perceptions of the value they believe libraries can offer them and there can be tensions between their requirements. Librarians and funding bodies do not always share the same set of value perceptions and in some library contexts, such as public libraries, this can become a political battlefield.

Creating segment-specific value propositions for stakeholders

Marketing planning for engagement in libraries will ensure that offers and messages are as specific as possible and reflect the values and tone of the various groups the library serves. Each type of library service should map its users and stakeholders (see Chapter 6). Stakeholders include students, lecturers, senior university managers (in academic libraries); adults, children, local government officers (in public libraries); doctors, nurses, patients, administrators (in health service libraries); staff in specific departments and levels of management (in corporate libraries).

In public libraries, librarians have grouped users and potential users who share similar wants and needs for more than a century in order to plan their services, though without calling such grouping segmentation. Groups have been based on a range of classifications, including materials (fiction, non-fiction, audiovisual and others), age group (children, teenagers and adults), type of use (local history, music, fiction, non-fiction) and ability (housebound or visually impaired, and requiring mobile services). In addition there are often good links with various communities of interest such as women's groups, parent teacher organisations, youth organisations and others. These are good examples of very basic, but also very useful, segmentation, where librarians recognise that users in each category may wish to access the whole range of library services but may have a very specific set of needs that only a public library service can satisfy.

Segmentation by value should provide the practical basis for service development in all types of libraries. It is the process of identifying groups of users and stakeholders who have similar needs, so they can be made distinct engaging offers, or service packages can be created for them. If this group is based on the area the user works in (e.g. business, voluntary sector) it is thought of as a market sector; if based on a complex mix of factors relating to lifestyle, life stage, age and value sought, it is a true segment.

Segmentation is an art rather than a science and there is no one true way to categorise your market. Look for a segmentation that will enable you to plan services better rather than simply to provide an academic or 'neat and tidy' picture of users and potential users. Effective segmentation helps librarians to identify and create the appropriate range of engaging services that must be provided if users are to find that the library provides something specifically for them and not just a service for all in some general way. Value is key to engagement.

Options for segmenting stakeholders

Figure 5.1 shows three ways to develop effective and practical division of library users: through behavioural, psychographic and profiling segmentation.

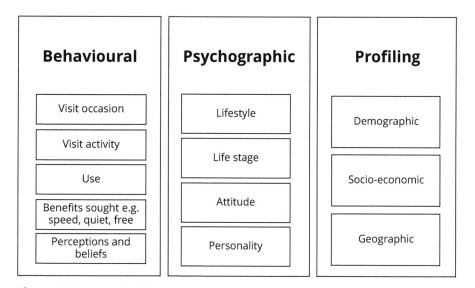

Figure 5.1 *Segmentation for engagement*

Segmentation based on simple profiles

Segmentation based on simple profiles (right-hand column of Figure 5.1), such as those provided by user profiling exercises, can be useful when evaluating how well a library is doing compared with funding body expectations by client group. If the funding body has an agenda to support a certain user or non-user group, reporting library activities by these specific groups is very appropriate. Marketing may well benefit from more sophisticated segmentation but it is always useful to have a clear understanding of the basic demographic, socio-economic and geographic characteristics of users and potential users.

Take an example from retail financial services to see why one factor alone is unlikely to be sufficient for effective segmentation. A priority group of interest to financial services companies may be, say, young professionals aged between 20 and 29. However, not all young professionals in their 20s have the same characteristics: some are married with children, some married without children, others are single and living alone or with contemporaries, and some live with their parents. One may currently be in a job with little current income but large potential income, another may have a sizeable income but no potential to increase it. Grouping these professionals by age in the context of what the financial services company is trying to do (sell) provides a useful basis for marketing strategy and engaging communication but this can be significantly improved by understanding the diversity of characteristics within the age category.

Although it can be valuable to report profiling figures to stakeholders such as funding and governance bodies, simple profiling is not immediately valuable when trying to engage users or potential users. Much more useful for this purpose are behavioural (looking at what people do) and psychographic (looking at what people think) segmentations.

Segmentation based on behavioural characteristics

Behavioural characteristics (left-hand column in Figure 5.1) are the basis for much market segmentation research in industry and commerce, and librarians would do well to investigate how people relate to libraries and use libraries. Behavioural requirements can be derived from such dimensions as occasion of visit, behaviour during visit, levels of use and perceptions and beliefs about library service. We can then sub-segment these where age, geography or other statistical profiling characteristics seem relevant.

Occasion of visit

A study of when people actually visit the library may well reveal some important information for segmentation and marketing of library services.

For example, if a group of people only visit the public library on a Thursday, perhaps because a bus only comes into the town centre on a Thursday, these library users are unlikely to be attracted into the library on other days of the week. Simply telling them more about the range of materials and services on offer is unlikely to lead them to visit the library more frequently.

A clear understanding of users' lifestyles, transport options and other factors may enable us to create a segment for which we reconfigure our offer if there are enough people within it to make it worthwhile. Obvious service developments would be to provide more remote access options for information and recreational uses of the library. Consequently, the marketing message to devise would be not simply, 'we have this material, come and use it', but rather, 'we understand your needs and your lifestyle and here is what we offer you, which is specifically created for you'. Notice that it is unlikely to be necessary to provide whole new services; instead, we need to ensure that the marketing messages that we send are well focused to user 'hot buttons' rather than just generalist, which may not engage library users. In the absence of segmentation, it is all too easy to fall back on sending one message to everybody, with perhaps a little tinkering around the edges when targeting who should be sent the message.

Level of use

Level of library use is a remarkably powerful behavioural characteristic that can form the basis of a 'quick win' segmentation for engagement. Every librarian knows that not all readers use the library in the same way or to the same level. Some readers come in every day and take out a large number of books. Others visit infrequently and only take out books occasionally. Some visit frequently but rarely borrow. If we categorise our existing users into three key groups – high use, medium use and low use – we have a useful segmentation for a 'quick win' in managing levels of engagement. Few people would doubt that the majority of next year's book issues are likely to come from existing users. Therefore if we understood which of these are heavy users, which are medium users and which are very light users we can focus our attention on where the easiest increase in issues is likely to come from. This categorisation can be used for all types of interaction with the library. It does not have to be solely related to issues of materials; for example, it could be applied to simple visits, attendance at events, and use of online services.

Our key marketing questions in such a segmentation relate to level of use:

■ *Heavy library users.* These are likely to be, but may not necessarily be, our most engaged users. What can they offer us? What will encourage them to remain such regular and frequent users? Are some of them likely to be our champions?

- *Medium library users*. Which of these users can we encourage to become heavy and highly engaged users? What would we have to do to increase their level of engagement? And how do we ensure that those who don't become heavy library users will remain medium library users? Are they fully engaged but already using the library to the level that they need?
- *Light library users*. Which light library users can be developed into medium or even heavy users? What would we have to do? Can we create engaging offers and messages to bring them closer to us? Are they fully engaged but already using the library to the level that they need?

Heavy library users have a relationship with the library and may want to develop it and be recognised as important users. Relationship marketing theory suggests that these users need to be treated differently from other groups because they are likely to be the bedrock of next year's library activity. They also have word-of-mouth marketing potential to spread a positive library message if they have appreciated any good service they received.

Given their importance to the future of the library service, we need to understand members of this highly engaged group in great detail and 'lock them in' to the service. Clearly there should be a different promotional campaign targeting this group than one that hopes to engage potential users. This should not be seen as unequal service. All segments should have a strong offer created for them that is relentlessly communicated. It is bad marketing practice simply to look for new users without also ensuring that already engaged users are understood, valued and communicated with in a way that recognises their previous relationship with the library. In marketing 'speak' this is known as balancing customer acquisition and customer retention.

Medium level users need a different marketing approach. We know that they use the library, but not frequently. With a little bit of research, it should be possible to create a number of engaging messages based on highly appropriate library service offerings. This may encourage a proportion of these medium level users to become more engaged with the library, perhaps increasing their library use, thus moving them into the heavy user category.

Research into low level users should again differentiate between those who will inevitably remain low level users because of lifestyle or other factors and those who might be encouraged to become significantly more engaged and frequent users. This is where the greatest engagement challenge is. Are they low users because their needs are already fully met and they do not feel the need for a closer relationship with the library, or are they unaware of the opportunities offered by the library and our messages are not engaging?

Segmentation based on psychographic characteristics

Perhaps the most important input to segmentation for engagement is psychological segmentation, which looks at lifestyle, life stages, attitude and personality. These are all based on feelings, hopes and fears that as human characteristics are potentially engaging or disengaging if perceived in a negative way. There is a close relationship with behavioural characteristics but here we are emphasising psychological aspects rather than simply factual activities.

Some library users may not be inspired by anything the library offers because of their lifestyle. If the library is to be relevant to them its offer, ambience and approach may have to change. Similarly, there are opportunities for engaging potential library users at different stages of their life (infancy, childhood, adolescence, youth, adulthood, old age) and through important rites of passage and life events (learning to read, enjoying childhood, establishing a career, having a family, caring for the old and making the most of retirement).

Effective segmentation is not easy . . .

Segmentation is not easy but creative library and information professionals craft combinations of all these factors to create a sound basis for developing engaging offers. To look beyond the simplistic categories such as age group, gender or socio-economic classification (in public libraries) or students, lecturers, courses (in academic libraries) requires a significant commitment to understanding the lifestyle and other changes that users and potential users frequently experience. If this commitment is not made you may find that your analysis of user and potential user value is inadequate for useful segmentation. Without a clear focus on value it is unlikely that you can be truly engaging for users and other stakeholders.

. . . but brings significant benefits

Segmentation underpins effective marketing planning. Librarians who group library users effectively are likely to have the most coherent and engaging marketing planning and communications processes. Nevertheless, segmentation inevitably reveals tensions. Many segmentation models quickly highlight the problem of meeting all the needs of various sectors within the same building or service.

Grouping users this way helps library managers make good choices. Consider which segments are:

■ most likely to help you to meet your objectives
■ most likely to engage with the library
■ inadequately serviced by competitors.

Which segments of your library users are most likely to help you to meet your objectives? All libraries have performance measures to meet, and (as noted in Chapter 2) marketing planning is not undertaken simply as a 'good thing' but rather as a means to achieving marketing objectives, for example through increases in issues, visits, enquiries or other activities and increasingly around more qualitative engagement measures and indicators. To simply undertake a comprehensive, general marketing campaign where everyone gets the same message is to assume all readers are equal. They may be equal in their entitlement to library service, but they are unlikely to be equal in the contribution they make to meeting library objectives or their responses to library offers. Segmentation enables you to identify groups most likely to deliver library objectives.

Which segments are most likely to engage with the library? A detailed understanding of user needs will reveal where our offer is most likely to be perceived as more or less attractive, and perhaps even irrelevant. There may be political reasons to market to some of those groups whose members do not immediately recognise or support the values inherent in library services, but it is more important to support the underlying health of the library service by encouraging high levels of engagement.

Which segments are inadequately serviced by our competitors? For example, although public library services are for all, there are some areas where the library provides a differential marketing advantage over alternative ways of meeting user needs. Users or potential users in segments whose needs are better met by the library than by any other provider are likely to respond more positively to library marketing communications than potential users in segments whose needs are met elsewhere. It may be worth prioritising a few key segments and positioning them as superior against competitive offers (probably non-library competitors for the same benefits). In an attempt to provide a service to all, public librarians can be tempted to take on competitors who are difficult to beat and then be surprised and disappointed when the library marketing effort seems ineffective.

Essentially, segmentation helps identify which groups of users are most likely to help the library meet its performance targets, whether quantified or qualitative. Perhaps the most important use of segmentation is to be the basis for creating a set of value propositions. Engagement requires a set of offers built around value, which can be taken to the library community market through a messaging campaign.

Value propositions by segment

Think about why people use libraries and what they value about library services. What do they get out of libraries and what do they truly value, compared with what librarians think is valuable about library services?

A value proposition describes how a library differentiates itself from competitors to users or potential users. It is the basis for creating an offer and is defined best by what they value:

> The customer never buys what the supplier sells. What is value to the customer is always something quite different from what is value or quality to the supplier.
>
> Drucker (2015)

This is an old, yet still important, marketing lesson for librarians and other professionals to learn. Are books and online databases valuable in themselves? How valuable is information? As effective marketing is based on a value proposition, library staff must be very clear what value the library has to offer. It is good to have a general value proposition for the library but far more engaging to have a set of value propositions by segment.

How users perceive value

There are perhaps three main questions at the back of a user or potential user's mind when they decide whether it is worth using library services:

- Are the library services offered to me worth the effort or price being charged?
- Do they help me to achieve things of importance to me?
- Is there a clear and compelling difference between the library's offer and other approaches to meeting my needs?

The first question might sound a little unusual to those librarians who are committed to providing a totally free library service. However, even where the library makes no direct charges there are costs for users, such as the time it takes to visit the library, transport fares and the opportunity cost of visiting the library rather than doing something else.

This brings us to the second question. Assuming there are no significant costs in visiting the library, it is extremely important that there is a positive reason for making a visit. If a visit does not help users achieve things of value to them, it is unlikely that advertising and promotional activity will be enough to attract them to try the service, let alone develop an engaging relationship over time.

Finally, the library may indeed help users achieve things of importance to them and the costs be worth the effort, but there may be a better way for users to meet their needs rather than take up the library's offer. In Chapter 4 we noted how there are many competitors with libraries for users' attention.

Although we may claim to have the best overall combination of services, facilities and collections to meet the generality of potential users, we need to develop value propositions by segment to prevent the overall offer falling into the middle ground, which may or may not really exist as a group to engage with.

Create value propositions for each segment

If we have positive responses to the three considerations discussed in the section above we can start to create a value proposition for each segment. It is fundamental to identify what value is to users in order to address it in advertising and promotional marketing activities. To be an effective marketer you may need to challenge your most basic beliefs about what value is. For example, is information valuable? Can you make a strong value proposition about the library's collection of printed and digital sources of information? Is the corporate library's collection of company and market research databases valuable? Does the set of wide-ranging databases of academic papers in academic libraries have value?

In fact, information has little or no value in itself; it tends to have value only in use. When information is stored as a collection or subscriptions are taken out to online databases it is best thought of as a cost because no value is created by its simple existence. While users or potential users may take some comfort from the fact that the library holds information, its real value for them is in what that material can help them achieve. Once this is understood, it becomes easy to present services in such an engaging way that you are clearly creating value for potential users. Simply to inform potential users of the materials the library has will not demonstrate to them that it is worth their while to visit it, except for those who are already aware of the library and know of the collection's value for them.

If library managers simply draw attention to a library's resources without clearly understanding and describing their value, they may be at risk of potential funding cuts. Collections of data and information have storage and maintenance costs; unless the value of a collection is recognised it may be seen to involve expensive running costs and be cut when times get hard.

Use Table 5.1 opposite to help you analyse the key dimensions of formulating value propositions by segment.

Table 5.1 *Analysis of a library's value to different segments of its user and potential user base*

	Segment 1	Segment 2	Segment 3 (etc.)
The library's value to this segment is			
The library helps this segment achieve the following things valuable to them			
This is why this segment should use the library rather than other ways to meet their needs			

Completing Table 5.1 should help you to define your value propositions. Then provide evidence that the value can indeed be transferred or acquired by using the library, and you are well on the way to having the source material for creating a convincing message to readers.

When filling in Table 5.1 remember that although the benefits users are looking for are achieved through library resources, the resources themselves are often not what the benefit is. For instance, a user might be planning to start a business (the benefit she is looking for), and she might use a library to help her achieve her goal because as a library user she has access to a range of excellent textbooks and referred contacts. She might prefer the library to the bookseller because the books are available on free loan; she might prefer the library to local government business support offices because the library staff, though less knowledgeable than the bookseller, are very friendly and helpful. Clearly it is now possible to think about the real value of the library service to this type of user and begin to define a value proposition that you can communicate through marketing channels. The offers that you make in the completed value proposition must be actionable by your library service and credible and compelling to those at whom the proposition is aimed.

It is useful to be able to point to stories of how people have used the library and as a result of that use have been able to achieve tasks of importance. If a picture is worth 1000 words then perhaps a story is worth 10,000 words. To reveal these stories ask your team to complete the following phrase for as many users as they know:

One day . . . came into the library and she/he . . ., which enabled her/him to . . .

In the first space give the real name of a real person (you are looking for individual stories not generalities); in the second space outline what the user's interaction with the library was; and in the third (most important) space state the outcome of the user's interaction with the library, for example:

- ■ 'One day David came into the corporate library and searched the company and market research databases and *left feeling well briefed on an aggressive competitor and their key markets.'*
- ■ 'One day Amira came into the public library and she was shown how to use the internet, which enabled her *to communicate with her family overseas.'*
- ■ 'One day Elizabeth came into the college library and borrowed some books on study skills, which helped *reduce her anxiety about writing her first assignment.'*
- ■ 'One day Abhay came into the hospital library to access the full range of information sources in his area of specialism and *left confident that his knowledge and research data would contribute to the literature.'*

The really engaging element is the third part of the sentence in italics. Although it is a good outcome from marketing if figures in a library demonstrate an increase in the number of people using databases or the internet, and borrowing books, these are not of themselves the most engaging activities in the minds of users. They are means to an end. In the examples above, feeling well briefed, communicating with family overseas, and reduction of anxiety are much more valuable. The alert marketer will aim to get messages such as these into any marketing communications rather than to fall back on merely describing what the service has – internet, books, displays and other things. Remember, it is not what the library has that matters but how these assets help users or potential users get to where they are trying to go.

Commit to collecting as many stories as possible of how users have benefited from engaging with the library. It is never a waste of time. The best advertising messages have a personal ring to them. Personal is engaging. Recommendations or testimonials are a powerful resource for developing an engaging marketing message.

Create personas to make segmentation data individual and vivid

Another way of analysing segmentation data is to create personas from the stories collected from users and research data on potential users. Personas are very brief descriptions of individuals that identify 'real' human beings, similar to those whom we might meet in the library or on the main street. They are not stereotypes (e.g. 'the young mother' or 'the undergraduate student') and should be described in sufficient detail to enable them to be recognised from a set of broad characteristics.

Here are four examples of the type of information that can help form personas:

- Matilda, age 49, part-time worker, very busy, involved in voluntary work, children have left home, interested in local history and is thinking of tracing her family tree, does not have a PC and keeps hearing about the internet from friends and magazines
- Baljinder, age 17, studying to enter higher education, very busy and gregarious, has internet at home, many friends and interests
- Derek, age 66, newly retired, enjoys gardening and music, worries about health and loneliness
- Ngozi, age 28, has a degree but not making progress in her career, two young children, interested in extreme sports but doesn't have time or money to indulge in them.

Notice that they have a specific age (rather than being stereotyped as teenagers or middle aged) and particular interests. It is useful to include a photograph with personas to make planning more personal and engaging. Such personas can be very useful in creating appropriate product and service packages and offers. IT companies often use personas when designing applications.

If you have segmented your market, understood the value that users in each segment are looking for and created a set of value propositions for each one, you can begin to develop your marketing communication strategy. You need to ensure that your value propositions are not simply well founded but also deliverable, and that you are committed to deliver them through appropriate engaging messages (see Chapter 8) and channels (see Chapter 9).

But first, now that we have understood users and grouped them by value it is time to consider the engagement of other stakeholder groups such as funding bodies and influencers (Chapter 6) and, taking all this into account, making some choices about users and other stakeholder groups to include in our strategic marketing plan for engagement (Chapter 7).

6

Managing stakeholder engagement

Effective engagement depends on positive management of a whole range of stakeholders. It is unlikely that simple direct messaging to those you want to engage with will be enough to develop deep engagement with them. Many libraries share a common core of stakeholders – funding body, employees, library users and potential users, and other external bodies, e.g. support groups, suppliers, the media – although each library service has some who are specific to their type of library. Managing the whole range of stakeholders creates an atmosphere and context that can be very supportive of your engagement activities. Many people like to feel they are part of a larger thing.

Within each stakeholder group there are likely to be a number of sub-groups worthy of consideration. For example, public libraries' funding stakeholders are likely to include local government organisations and organisations that offer grants, while academic libraries' funding stakeholders are likely to include the university, those who have made bequests and grant awarding bodies. Employee stakeholders are managers, frontline staff and sometimes volunteers.

Most variation is likely to be found in the users and potential users category. Health service libraries have user stakeholders from a wide range of disciplines – clinicians, through nurses to general practitioners and administrative staff. Health services user groups are further complicated by the professions allied to health, which may have different engagement triggers to take account of. Business and corporate libraries have a complex mix of stakeholders from senior management teams to project teams. This complexity of users as stakeholders was considered in Chapter 5.

Three elements of a stakeholder management programme

All non-user stakeholder groups need to be engaged if possible in order to get their funding and organisational support. Essentially there are three key elements within a stakeholder management programme – identification, analysis and communications management – which are discussed below.

Identify stakeholders

When identifying stakeholders of a library who would be suitable to be involved in a stakeholder management programme think about all the people affected by the library's work or who are interested in the success or otherwise of its goals. Brainstorm a list as a starter and circulate it for others to comment on and add to. As you network, campaign or lobby through your advocacy activities note any individuals or organisations that seem especially influential in the areas you wish to engage with. The following groups may potentially be supportive stakeholders:

- Library suppliers may be a source of seed funding or provide introductions to other influential people. Their continued existence depends on selling items to libraries so be very clear about the benefits they will receive for helping you with your user engagement strategy.
- Policy-making organisations may be within and beyond your library funding body. These organisations need help with implementing their strategies and goals. If you can align with them there is significant opportunity for mutual benefit.
- Trade and professional associations and industry groups may not be a source of finance but they can often engage and act as advocates for activities that are consistent with their own aims and values.
- Philanthropists and philanthropy groups are often sympathetic to the work of libraries.
- Individual people of influence have sometimes benefited from libraries on their way to success or see libraries as a potential tacit supporter of a cause they champion. This category can include anyone, from a successful business person to a famous celebrity. University libraries in particular may well benefit if they seek help from their alumni organisation.
- Local cultural and other institutions, although often underfunded themselves, can often create supportive messages for local libraries, which add depth to your engagement activities. They will be keen to get you to support their events – an appropriate association between local cultural institution and local library can lead to users and stakeholders being engaged with each other.

After reflection you will find a large array of potentially helpful stakeholders for whatever type of library you are. However, not all stakeholders are equal.

Analyse stakeholders for engagement potential

The purpose of this stage is to ensure we understand stakeholders in the things that matter to us – their power to make or influence decisions together with their interest in library service and its outcomes. The outcome you seek is to persuade a range of stakeholders to work individually and together to support your wider engagement activities.

Decide for each of your stakeholders how powerful they are and what their level of interest in the library is, using your best estimations – it is the relativities that matter not the absolute placing. Each stakeholder has some degree of power to influence library funding, and some interest in the library vision and how it aligns with their future. When analysing the potential of stakeholders, note any attitudes they have shown towards the library – positive or negative.

Then you can use Figure 6.1 to show you what engagement approach to use for different categories of stakeholder according to their level of interest in the library and their power, and draw up a set of priorities for each of them. Some people prefer to create a scoring grid to help a wider team agree positioning but this is not strictly necessary. Include even the stakeholders who you have plotted as your lowest priority for engaging within your communications policy and plan.

	Power	
	High	**Low**
High	Regular contact to inform, persuade and remind	Keep informed
Low	Look for ways to increase their interest if attitude is positive	Stay alert to any increase in power or opportunity to increase interest

(Interest axis labelled on the left: **High** / **Low**)

Figure 6.1 *Engagement approach for different categories of stakeholder according to their level of interest in the library and their power*

Work out an engagement approach and communications plan for each stakeholder

Consider each stakeholder's position as it falls in Figure 6.1 to guide your engagement approach for them:

■ *High power and high interest.* Powerful and influential stakeholders deserve your sustained attention so they are fully engaged with your goals if at all possible. Provided their interest in library service is positive (they align with its vision, values and goals) and not negative (e.g. they see it as a competitor to their own interests or a source for spending cuts), devote time to crafting powerful value-driven, engaging messages for these stakeholders.

■ *High power with lower levels of interest.* Undertake further analysis of what powerful stakeholders who are less interested in your library are trying to achieve. Keep an open dialogue with them, and where possible align your library goals with theirs so you can craft engaging communications for them. Always look for opportunities to build their interest in library topics. Unless you have an engaging message for these stakeholders do not overburden them with frequent communication as it will be counterproductive. If you send them a message which they deem to be irrelevant, they may well ignore the next message you send them.

■ *Low power but highly interested in the library and its goals.* Keep stakeholders who have little power but a keen interest in the library informed of library service developments and activities. As they are probably already engaged your messages are likely to have a positive response. However, do not be tempted to spend an inordinate amount of time with this group as they may have little influence where funding or other supportive decisions are made. Undoubtedly when times are difficult a conversation with such positive people can reinvigorate and re-energise those who are responsible for the engagement programme.

■ *Low power with low levels of interest.* Monitor stakeholders in this group and should any of them increase in power look for ways in which to spark their interest (usually by aligning library activity with their goals). Do not expect much engagement from this group but stay alert to opportunities and occasionally inform them of library developments.

When devising messages and communication plans consider the following for each stakeholder:

■ What financial or emotional interest do they have in the outcomes of library activities? If they are likely to be interested in library service make sure to inform them of any changes to your current provision.

- What is their current attitude towards the library and the services it provides? Has their experience so far been positive? If not, what will win their hearts and minds back to support your engagement projects? And if you think their view will remain negative how will you manage that?
- What are their key motivators? Use the language of these motivators in your communications.
- Can they get what the library offers from elsewhere? If not then you are in a good position. If they can, use persuasive language to tempt them to consider using the library.
- What are their favoured channels for communication? Speak where they will listen.

Recognising the differences between stakeholder motivations and potential for engagement and support in your projects is more important than looking for similarities. Do not be tempted to look for one message to all. It takes time, a great deal of reflection and sustained activity to develop relationships.

Figure 6.2 shows key ways in which you can engage with stakeholders; you can create a custom mix for each stakeholder. Notice that there is not an option to 'ignore' them. All stakeholders deserve to be part of your planning even if only for an occasional message.

Although the highest level of engagement is collaborating, this is extremely time-consuming and unlikely to be used for all stakeholders. More likely the key activities are going to be around messaging key specific communications

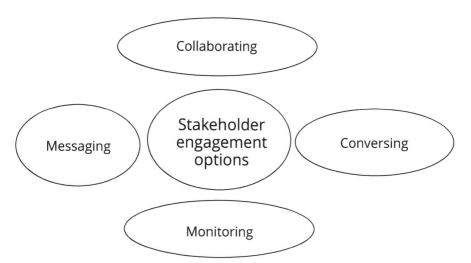

Figure 6.2 *Ways to engage stakeholders*

to each stakeholder, staying alert to the possibility of turning these contacts into ongoing conversations. It may take some time before there is enough understanding and trust between you and the stakeholder to discuss real collaborations. However, along the way there may be some key learning that you can use to develop wider engagement within the library community. The most important thing is to engage to whatever level is realistic and appropriate. Passive relationships are very rarely appropriate even where the stakeholder has a degree of negativity towards the library service. Keeping quiet simply feeds into the notion of the library as being a best kept secret or confirms the reasons for the stakeholder's negativity.

Once you have identified a small number of stakeholders to give special attention because you feel there are genuine and mutually beneficial opportunities in investigating some joint collaborations:

■ Be clear what you can achieve from the partnership or collaboration. Inevitably there will be areas of vision and values where you may need to compromise. Which areas can you compromise on and which are absolutely sacrosanct?
■ Look for the creative. The more interesting a collaboration is the more likely that energy will be sustained to drive it.
■ Be clear what you have to offer the partner. Even if they are philanthropic it is good to show clear benefits to them.
■ Be patient – relationships develop slowly.

Consider the wider stakeholder environment and assess the potential for engaging with broader national or international initiatives. For example, in the UK a number of universities have signed up to the National Co-ordinating Centre for Public Engagement (www.publicengagement.ac.uk) to investigate ways to engage the public with university activities and research. If academic libraries in contributing institutions can find ways to support their institution's activities, internal stakeholders are likely to engage with them positively.

Having identified your key external stakeholders and reflected on how they can help you to meet your engagement objectives complete Table 6.1 opposite.

Completing the simple stakeholder analysis chart shown in Table 6.1 (which needs a supporting detailed action plan) will focus your attention on who the major stakeholders of your library are, what you need from them and your strategy to engage them. Engaging with stakeholders is key to your future (because of their influence on funding or governing bodies) but has potential risks as well as benefits. Be sure to manage the relationships sensitively and carefully as risks and rewards are high. You are more likely

Table 6.1 *Analysis of stakeholders, what they offer the library, and engagement strategies and actions*

Stakeholder	Power (high or low)	Interest (high or low)	What do we need from them?	Engagement strategy and actions

to be successful in your engagement strategy if you are able to give the stakeholder something in return. Reciprocity is one of the key sources of influence and persuasion.

Engaging employees

A key part of stakeholder management is employee engagement. People tend to engage with people rather than things. If your employees are not engaged with their jobs and the organisation then why should users and other stakeholders be engaged?

It is likely that some of your employees are fully engaged with, and inspired by, your values and programmes, some are neutral and some are actively disengaged. Support and recognise your engaged employees, inspire and energise your neutral staff, and understand and manage your actively disengaged staff to the point where they either become engaged or should consider why they are working for you.

After all, your employees are one of the key stakeholder groups to manage in pursuit of effective engagement in your library community. They deliver the promises you make and as the frontline that is where users' experience is judged. Uninspired and de-motivated employees can quickly unravel all the hard work you have put into an engagement programme.

Employee engagement is measured by the extent to which employees feel passionate about their jobs, are committed to the library service, and go beyond what is strictly necessary when dealing with library users, potential users or other stakeholders. Positive engagement is much more than simple employee satisfaction – employees' basic happiness, contentedness concerns and needs. However, bear in mind that it might be difficult to establish an inspired and motivated team if employees' basic needs and happiness are not considered.

As with all things, reflect on what employee engagement means for your library and whatever models you adopt be alert to the adaptions that might be necessary for your workplace. Employees are likely to be cynical if they see employee engagement strategies and plans as simply a copycat template derived from some human resources or talent management consultancy. You are trying to win hearts and minds – not an easy task in our diverse and fragmented world. Trust, fairness, values and respect are likely to be important components of employee engagement, especially how employees feel that they are treated by their direct supervisor.

To kick-start an employee engagement project remember the virtues of quick wins and sincerity. You will easily be found out if this simply becomes a tick box exercise with some mysterious pay off in the long-term future, which never seems to get any closer.

These are some quick wins you might aim to achieve:

- Create a brief employee engagement survey or focus groups with a commitment to review and act on the results in the near future.
- Invite employees to submit ideas that will engage them and the library community.
- Use team building activities to investigate and encourage engagement.
- Recognise engagement in some way.

Always remember context. For example, your library service may recently have suffered significant funding restrictions that have de-motivated staff. Demotivation and disengagement are two separate, though sometimes related, issues.

Longer term, commit to review staff appraisal systems to reflect your engagement metrics and ensure that engagement behaviour is rewarded. Review internal communication so that employees feel an important part of library goals. As well as developing organisation-wide strategies, ensure direct managers recognise their critical contribution to staff engagement (Table 6.2).

Table 6.2 *How direct managers and organisational managers can engage employees*

Direct manager's role in engagement strategies	Organisational manager's role in engagement strategies
Earn trust by being open and vulnerable (admit mistakes, listen to feedback)	Set the tone for line managers to encourage engagement
Have regular conversations about what is working, what is not. Ask 'how can I help you?'	Involve everyone in the real purpose and values of the organisation
Open opportunities for staff to use their creativity and skills	Keep everyone aware of the progress of the organisation and celebrate success
Actively search and plan for development opportunities	Frequently ask employees for their improvement ideas
Show recognition (check what works for staff . . . often it is not money alone)	Have an annual staff development plan that you stick to

Bring out the best in each employee. Appreciate their efforts and you have a fighting chance of good engagement. The detail is what makes a strategy powerful. When you have identified the key staff engagement issues that you need to put in place to support your library community engagement activities, identify a series of goals and support them with an action plan, as shown in Table 6.3.

Table 6.3 *Action plan to develop employee engagement*

	Employee engagement goal 1	Employee engagement goal 2	Employee engagement goal 3
Action to engage staff in this goal			
Who is responsible for the actions?			
When will it happen and be completed?			
Resource required			
How will we judge success?			
When will success or other outcomes be discussed and next steps agreed?			

In the quest for developing effective engagement strategies you have now added stakeholder understanding and management to your analysis. The next chapter looks at the choices that arise as you develop engaging offers.

7

Making choices and creating engaging offers

By now in the process of marketing planning for engagement you will have an emerging set of opportunities for engagement activity. Having set ambition (Chapter 3), reflected on users' and potential users' needs and wants (Chapter 4), identified the value the library can offer, and segmented library markets into practical groups of users (Chapter 5), and looked for stakeholders to help create and deliver a library offer to each segment (Chapter 6) you can now choose where the library can make the most impact. Then the library can attend to finalising engaging offers.

Unfortunately there will not be enough financial and other resources to implement all your ideas and you have to choose which engagement options to develop into detailed strategies and action plans. Making decisions and choices within a wide analytical planning framework can be done at many levels. Some library staff simply reflect the current priorities of their funding body and ensure it is supported by a detailed action plan reflecting the vocabulary and language of the funding bodies. Others take a broader view.

Priorities

Library and information professionals are often creative, and there is no shortage of ideas to develop and market libraries. However, there is never enough time or money to do everything that library managers would like to do all at once. If priorities are not set then there is a danger that the library resorts to the easiest or most interesting activities rather than addresses difficult issues which have the greatest potential impact and urgency.

It can be daunting to set priorities if they have not already been set by the top team who makes decisions on library funding. Where do you start? These are some of the most important questions to consider for those setting priorities:

- What are the fundamental activities members of the funding body believe that the library has to do? What is the library 'in business' to do? An existing mission–vision–values statement should be of considerable use here.
- Which activities contribute most to the library achieving that value to its stakeholders?
- What are the clear outcomes that demonstrate excellence? There are likely to be a mix of quantitative and qualitative indicators. Activities that clearly show excellence have more impact than those that simply maintain the library's current position.
- What is the library's unique contribution to the success of the organisation? What are the things that will not be done unless the library does them?
- Where does the library save money or create more value?
- Where is the best return on investment in people, time and money?

Engagement objectives

Objectives are 'what' we want to achieve and we use strategies to achieve them. Marketing objectives, like all other objectives, should be SMART – specific, measurable, achievable, realistic and time specific.

If the objective is to increase engagement then it should be accompanied by pre- and post-campaign measurement of the variables you have used to define engagement. A vague objective to increase engagement is not a good driver for either marketing or engagement strategy. Objectives can be set at either service-wide or segment level. It is best to have both.

Objectives are not scientific but set to achieve a desired state, though they are often quantified. Sometimes objectives are qualitative, for example a library might have the objective to improve stakeholders' opinions of the library service. This objective is measured by considering how stakeholders' opinions of the library have changed since they were first collected or over the last year.

See Chapter 11 for advice on evaluation of engagement objectives and strategies.

Engagement strategies

An engagement strategy sets out engaging offers and undertakes a programme of action to reach a future desired state, for example, how to take a library service from the present to its vision of the future. A useful first stage in this strategy setting process is to undertake a From-To-Analysis where members of the senior management team, with input from members of frontline teams, identify key dimensions of their vision of what engagement is, identify the current position and outline the changes required to achieve the future position (Table 7.1). Having identified the required action necessary during the planning period or beyond, the team should set out clearly what will be necessary to ensure the action is successful and any difficulties or risks that arise, including initial thoughts on how to mitigate them. To take an example, there may be a library engagement strategy to change the key stakeholders' view of the library within the organisation from a neutral position to a more positive, actively supportive one. This could require a change from letting the library be seen as a 'best kept secret' to publicising its presence. The change can be made by undertaking a thorough stakeholder analysis, then using an understanding of the issues and policies that influence stakeholders to create and implement a campaign to align with them. Clearly there are risks in raising the library's profile, as once raised the library will be seen as an unambiguous contributor to the value the organisation creates.

Table 7.1 *A From-To-Analysis: how to get from where we are currently to where we want to go*

From	To	Changes required	How will we make the changes?	Issues and risks to manage

Key issues and risks might be how to manage this campaign to ensure that the library shows real value and does not simply publicise its presence as an asset, which can be cut if times get hard; staff resistance to any changes required; and a lack of marketing planning skills to develop the required user understanding. These might be mitigated by ensuring the campaign is clearly aligned with stakeholder concerns, and introducing change management programmes for staff, and staff training in marketing planning tools and techniques.

Four strategies to generate engagement
Not all users and potential users offer the same opportunity for successful engagement. One way to illustrate this is to use an adapted form of the Ansoff

matrix, a strategic planning tool, to highlight the relative openness to engagement that you might encounter when creating offers and messages for various types of user and potential user. Figure 7.1 shows the adapted matrix, setting out how to engage existing and new library users with existing and new offers.

The four strategies are discussed below.

Offer (Products/services)

	Existing	**New**
Existing	Increase use of existing offer by existing group(s)	Make a new offer to existing group(s)
New	Find new group(s) of users to use existing offer	Set up a new offer for a group that does not currently use the library

(row/column label: **User or non-user segment**)

Figure 7.1 *Matrix setting out how to engage existing and new users with existing and new offers*

Market penetration strategy

Generate more engagement from existing user segments by communicating and promoting existing products and services. This is a market penetration strategy for engagement and the least risky of the four alternatives. It is likely to be the most successful approach as existing users already have some degree of engagement with you. You are likely to have a good understanding of this group and the current range of products and services the library offers. Stakeholders in this segment who do not currently use the library are likely to engage with your offer as you have a good understanding of their needs and a history of success with the products and services offered in the past to groups like them.

Market extension strategy

Generate more engagement from communicating and promoting existing products and services to new segments who currently do not use the library.

This is a market extension strategy for engagement whereby you use existing products and services to extend the market, without developing new offerings. It is appropriate where you believe there are potential users who might start using the library if they only knew about it and how it could benefit them. Market extension strategies are useful when you understand your products and services well and are able to deliver them in full, but you have limited knowledge of potential users and no close relationship historically, so engagement is far from a natural activity.

The risk to a market extension strategy is that you do not understand the user segment enough and mistakenly believe your standard offer is likely to be a winner with them. One size does not fit all. For market extension strategies to be successful you must be aware of the important, perhaps small, differences between potential user groups which do not currently take up your offer. Slight alteration or customisation may be the difference between success or failure.

New product development strategy

Generate more engagement from developing new products and services for existing user segments. Where you believe that deeper engagement with existing user segments is important to your future, develop a new product development strategy. Use your close understanding of the needs, lifestyles and other segmentation variables of these user groups to look for innovative and attractive new service delivery or content. Sometimes you can offer an entirely new type of material, sometimes you can find new ways to distribute library services, perhaps from afar or digitally.

Diversification strategy

Generate new engagement by developing new products and services for new user segments. A diversification strategy for engagement is the riskiest type of strategy but has the potential to transform an organisation. However, in the current marketing world diversification is not considered an attractive engagement strategy as it takes an organisation into new areas, where the needs and wants of stakeholders are not understood well enough to allow an organisation to predict confidently the response to its offers. Such an understanding cannot be achieved simply by surveying new groups and responding to what they say they want. Furthermore, the new products and services developed may, at best, stretch the competencies and capabilities of the organisation or, at worst, take it into areas where it is unlikely to deliver its offer. Despite being risky, public libraries are sometimes instructed or choose to create this risky marketing strategy, with limited, and often transient, success.

Crafting a mix of strategies

Having identified four strategy options for generating engagement it is necessary to craft a relevant mix of strategies. Will all new engagement activity be directed towards new users for instance? Or 50% from new users and 50% from existing users? Or 75% from existing users? Think about what your ambitions are and use Figure 7.1 to decide what proportion of engagement activity to allocate in each section of the grid, so the total is 100%. This will force you to align your objectives and strategies. Once you are clear what proportion of new engagement activity each strategy will generate, it is easier to choose marketing communications and promotions.

After all this reflection and analysis it is nearly time to choose priority segments and where to direct engagement efforts. Strong, winning offers have to be based around a value proposition for each chosen segment, but before you create the offers think about what the opportunities are for the library. Is the library strong enough to beat alternatives to your service or is it too weak for its offer to be engaging?

To understand this more consider undertaking a SWOT analysis, looking at strengths, weaknesses, opportunities, threats (Table 7.2). This is a very well known analytical exercise and some of you will have compiled them in the past. SWOT analyses are easy to brainstorm and can give you a broad overview of what those involved in the analysis think of the library. Their

Table 7.2 *A SWOT analysis for a public library*

Strengths	Weaknesses
• Free service • Access to computers • Range of databases • Friendly staff • Strong service ethos • Some unique collections • Keen to adapt around user lifestyles	• Variable quality stock and staff • Public perception not always aligned with librarians • Very variable marketing and advocacy skills • Highly political funding bodies • Modesty (best kept secret) • Still struggling with clearly outlining return on investment for the community
Opportunities	**Threats**
• Support initiatives as they appear (e.g. health information) • Become advocates for digital literacy and facts • Use library spaces in creative ways (e.g. maker spaces, 'let's move in libraries')	• Potential for funding cuts • Large number of alternative suppliers of information and recreational needs • Political uncertainty • Staying invisible without influence • Increased automation removing the human element supporting engagement

downsides are that a simple brainstorming can sometimes result in an analysis so bland it is in effect useless in helping you choose segments to create winning offers for, and your view of your library's strengths and weaknesses may not tally with the view of those for whom you are about to create offers.

The SWOT analysis shown in Table 7.2 can be made even more specific when undertaken for a specific library authority, but to make the SWOT analysis really interesting for any type of library it should be performed by segment: by groups of library users, potential users or other stakeholders rather than for the library service as a whole. Should you undertake the analysis at whole library level you are unlikely to get useful guidance from it to help you choose segments for offer development.

Set out strengths, weaknesses, opportunities and threats on a graph as shown in Figure 7.2, with two axes – 'potential benefit to us' (your conclusions from considering opportunities and strengths in this segment) and 'ability to achieve' (considering the weaknesses and threats to your potential in this segment). When all segments are plotted you can see the relative potential of each one and can decide which segments will deliver the most return for the amount of effort and other resource you have to expend in order to create, advertise and deliver a winning offer.

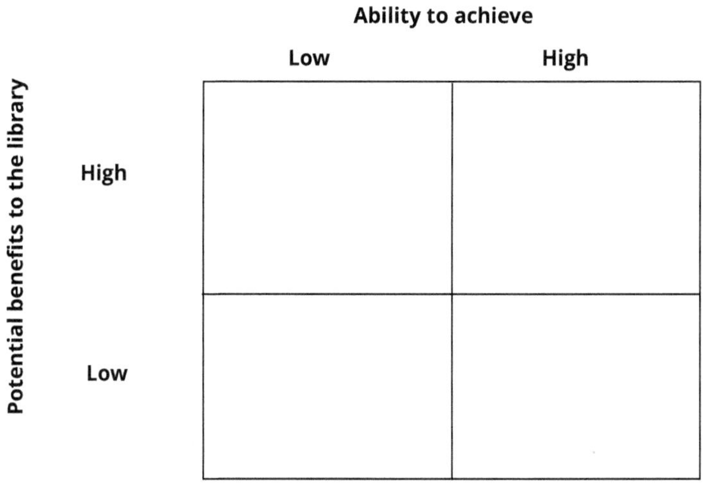

Figure 7.2 *Analysis of library opportunities by ability to achieve them and potential benefit*

With these choices made it is time to devise 'offers' within an overall strategy for engagement.

Creating offers for users, potential users and stakeholders

There are three main types of engagement strategies for libraries:

- general service-wide marketing strategies
- segment-specific marketing strategies
- user and stakeholder experience management strategies.

General service-wide marketing strategies create a basic marketing infrastructure that is strong enough to support a series of engaging segment-specific offers. This level includes the management of brand and sub-brands, ensuring that the brand is neither too general to be of interest to anyone in particular nor too specific to potentially distance or exclude key user segments. Engagement is often very much driven by brand. Potential users or supportive other stakeholders are often more likely to be persuaded to engage with a library because they feel positive about the idea of being associated with it than because they have made a dispassionate evaluation of the pros and cons of engaging with it.

Segment-specific strategies configure an offer around the value proposition developed for each segment. User experience strategies take these segment offers and ensure they are engaging for the segment.

With the broad library strategy in place you now need to move on to create very detailed strategies for individual segments (existing and new), which can be supported by a tactical one-year marketing plan. This strategy development includes creating engaging offers based on the elements of the marketing mix. 'Offers' should combine services that library staff believe will be the physical manifestation of the value proposition for the segment.

Traditionally marketing offers have been developed around a marketing mix of Product, Price, Place, Promotion (the four Ps). Others have turned these around and described them from the customer's point of view as Customer needs, Cost, Convenience, Communication (the 4Cs). Consultancies and academics have added other Ps over the years, such as Process Packaging, People and Physical evidence. Libraries might like to consider Politics and Partnerships as extra Ps, making at least a 6P model, as these are often encouraged and necessary for financial reasons as well as political concerns in some library authorities. Other Ps could be added, such as Perceptions. Include those that you believe make a difference in your library environment, but do not slavishly copy external models as these generic approaches are unlikely to inspire either your staff or others you wish to engage with.

In recent years there has been some dissatisfaction with the traditional marketing mix model and the emphasis has shifted to relationship marketing where organisational strategy is driven by one-to-one relationships with individual customers rather than mass marketing to a general customer base. Library strategy and the resulting offers should include a statement of the type of relationship you want with the segment. Some segments do not benefit from a close relationship with the library (perhaps because they do not feel the need to have one), while others prefer to have a close relationship. Levels of potential engagement vary significantly.

Whether the library service sets out its strategy at a very general level or, preferably, at a detailed segment or even one-to-one (customer relationship management) level it should consider its offers as they fit within a 6P (product, price, place, promotion, partnerships, politics) or similar marketing mix. We now look at each element in detail.

The marketing mix
Product (user needs)

It is essential to decide what products and services to provide as part of the modern library service and how to offer them to users and potential users. One can think of the options as a 'pizza of products and services' (Figure 7.3), which should meet the needs and wants of all legitimate and potential users. Our general strategy would be to make sure that all this is in place, and for marketing purposes the segment-specific communications strategy would be to reconfigure the pizza slices into dishes for the specific segments. This

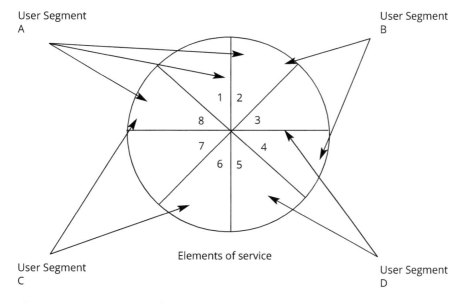

Figure 7.3 *Service elements of a segment-specific communications strategy*

usually requires strong marketing of only part of the service to each user segment, while perhaps gently informing those in them of the wider range of materials on offer. The aim is to engage people, not confuse them with too many potential library benefits all at once.

In Figure 7.3 the 'pizza' circle represents the set of products and services that the library service offers to satisfy the broad range of user needs. The general marketing strategy is to keep this infrastructure in place. More powerful marketing strategies are those by segment that focus on the key elements of service required by each user or other stakeholder segment. For instance, Segment A is only particularly interested in three slices of the library pizza. While there is always the potential to cross-sell into other slices the most powerful marketing to attract Segment A will be to provide an offer around the three slices it is most likely to engage with, which can then be communicated with a strong message. Segment A's needs are only met by service elements 1, 2 and 8. To market elements 3–7 to Segment A is to present the users in this segment with potentially irrelevant messages which do more harm than good.

A notable exception would be where Segment A is already making full use of the three parts of the service that fit its value proposition and is unlikely to be stimulated into extra use regardless of the persuasiveness of your marketing message. In such instances cross-selling to other slices might be a potential strategy, but one that is unlikely to be successful unless the segment genuinely wants and needs the benefits of other parts of the service. And if that were the case the library service should have identified this during the research phase for the creation of the value proposition.

Price (cost)

Even where there is a strong commitment to free service with no charge or fee for any aspect of provision it would be foolish to think that there are no costs involved for users. As noted earlier, there may be transport, time and energy costs (including users' experience in dealing with the bureaucracy of many library processes) or other opportunity costs for users when considering using library services.

These are some of the key questions to be addressed:

■ Can you deliver a full value proposition without charging fees for at least part of the offer? A part fulfilment for free is not necessarily going to be acceptable if it is a value proposition that is only engaging when delivered on time in full and is so expensive to deliver that it cannot be offered without a direct fee.

- How can users' costs in using the service be reduced? Can new ways to deliver services be found which are more convenient to them, for example through new delivery channels or extended opening hours? Make it easy and inexpensive to engage.
- Are you aware of the relative costs and value to users of using the competition such as bookshops and online services?

Place (convenience)

The 'place' element of the marketing mix is all about the channels or routes to market needed to deliver efficient and effective service to users. In public libraries, for instance, it is most obviously seen in the number and location of branches and mobile libraries but modern approaches consider 'place' to be more than a physical location. Place can be any way of delivering service: static, remote or online.

As with product you will have a set (pizza) of routes to market that will enable you to offer users convenient access to the product and services on offer. Certain user categories may need to have particular routes to market clearly outlined. For example, business people away from home for several nights every week may prefer to access services remotely while in hotels rather than through static service points when they return.

Promotion and advocacy (communication)

Promotion and advocacy can be a mix of advertising, sales promotions, public relations and attendance at events or visiting specific client groups to discuss the library and its services. Some segments require a strategy that does little more than inform or remind. Others require a persuasive promotional one that includes inducements to try the library service. Potential users are unlikely to be bribed into the library and you should not expect offers of free services to be successful unless the overall offer is right. A good principle to follow is that 'free stuff' should be offered as a reward to existing library users to encourage more library use. Non-users usually require a more engaging offer than free services, although such an offer could trigger the first use of the library.

Politics

Libraries are subject to political processes, whether they are in the public, academic, health service or corporate sector. They are likely to have changing political leaders and must create and communicate engaging marketing messages to each stakeholder.

This political dimension to library engagement strategies has become increasingly important in an era where the question 'whose side are you on?' appears to be prevalent among members of political parties and users of social media, and the notion that 'we can agree to disagree' is less common than in the past. When attempting to be highly engaging be very aware that what may be an attractive message to one group of people may be anathema to others.

Partnerships

Libraries have always sought close relationships with organisations with whom they share a similar or complementary vision. It is unlikely that large sums of investment money will be directed solely at libraries in the near future, so joint bids for funds with partners is an appropriate marketing strategy. Additionally, partners can sometimes add weight to the library offer for particular segments.

A partnership strategy is likely to help when delivering an engagement and marketing plan. Partnerships can be formed with other similar organisations or, more innovatively, with organisations from very different sectors. As previously noted, alignment of values and outcomes sought is crucial for these partnerships to retain the energy to be effective.

Beware of forming partnerships for the general good that turn out to be time-consuming without showing quick benefits. Partnerships benefit from having specific goals, whether as a learning or a service alliance. They can support your engagement and marketing strategy and plan as partners in funding, research, building audiences, developing and delivering services, and training. Inevitably they can be difficult to manage, with issues of power and trust.

Engagement and customer relationship management as a strategy

Engagement in libraries is a strategy based on employing user information in a sustained and focused manner to attract and retain library users through ongoing, meaningful conversations that build long-lasting, mutually beneficial relationships.

All elements of this definition are important, especially the final clause – mutually beneficial relationships. Relationship or engagement marketing is founded on users and the library service achieving measurable benefits.

Customer relationship management involves a series of tools and techniques as well as technology. It is easy to buy technology from vendors but without using it correctly you will not achieve the benefits that the approach can bring. Before you embark on an engagement or customer relationship management project be absolutely sure you know what you expect it to deliver, and how it can and will be delivered. Only then look for technology vendors who can provide what you need. Treat off the shelf packages with caution.

As noted in Chapter 4, not all readers are the same. Customer relationship management offers the potential to provide a personalised service that is based on having a deep understanding of users. You could send existing users regular e-mail updates of new additions to the library, based on their past borrowing or usage habits or expressed preferences. Customer relationship management for non-users emphasises customer service and offer development.

Whether such personalisation for engagement is worthwhile depends on a number of factors:

- *Diversity of user needs.* Where user needs are very similar among individuals within a segment, personalisation of the overall offer will not deliver great benefits for either the individual or the library service. However, when there are significant differences within a segment there are benefits in personalising the service within it. For instance, if the segment is disability the service should be personalised to reflect the unique needs of each person in the segment.
- *Distribution of lifetime values.* If all members of a particular segment have similar visit, issue, enquiry or political potential for the library service bear this factor in mind when considering service personalisation. Clearly if potential is the same across the segment then extra effort may not bring extra return. Similarly if one segment has a significantly higher potential return than another it may be worth considering personalising the service to attract those within it.
- *Ease of tailoring the offer and interactions.* Inevitably there are significant barriers to tailoring library services, which can be complex and expensive, and it is difficult to manage expectations. If barriers are high then the benefits from any tailoring may be low. When assessing the potential for personalisation consider whether the offer, the message or both should be personalised. It is perfectly reasonable in some circumstances to personalise the message but not the offer.

To undertake effective customer relationship management as part of your engagement and marketing plan you need:

■ *A database of user contacts and activity.* Personalising the offer, message or service relationship can only be undertaken in the context of an excellent information base on users and potential users.

■ *Analyses of the database.* The database is of no practical use unless tools exist to analyse the information and look for meaningful patterns that can influence offer development, marketing communications or service delivery.

■ *Relationships with targeted users.* A commitment to a sustained programme to build relationships is required. Without developing such relationships over time the programme is unlikely to have any purpose, impact or outcome.

■ *Privacy policies.* Customer relationship management is a very data intensive approach to developing service. Users are unlikely to allow you to collect data about them unless they are convinced that it is safe with you. Trust is key. Engagement requires trust. Customer relationship management requires engagement.

■ *Metrics.* Customer relationship management involves creating mutually beneficial relationships so monitor and measure that these benefits accrue as expected, for example to measure cost of providing new services to users, users' satisfaction levels, staff response levels, complaint levels, call answering times, response times to enquiries. See Chapter 11 for an overview of engagement evaluation activities.

Finalising engaging offers for specific segments

Now that you have considered the marketing mix model (via a 6P, or similar, approach) and the issues behind relationship marketing it is time to create a distinct offer for each segment of the market, as discussed in Chapter 5. There are certain segments where you want not just a good offer but the winning offer, for example where support for, and engagement with, the segment is very important to the future health of the library service. The differences between the defined offers for individual segments have significant implications for developing your engaging marketing communications (Chapter 8).

To create an engaging offer for each segment you bring together your understanding of segmentation with your knowledge of the value proposition and the marketing and relationship mix for each one. Good marketing customises the service around a key marketing mix infrastructure and uses relationship marketing tools and techniques. The main decision is how to create a balance of marketing mix and relationship strategies to meet the engagement and marketing objectives.

Table 7.3 sets out the points to consider when devising an engagement marketing strategy for different library segments.

Table 7.3 *Points to consider when devising an engagement marketing strategy for different library segments*

	Segment A	Segment B	Segment C (etc.)
Product or service			
Price, or costs reduced for user or potential user			
Key ways to access the product or service (place)			
Promotional activity			
Political considerations			
Partners in the offer and their contribution			
Relationships strategy (how close to the segment are we?, how close do we want to be?)			

Complete Table 7.3 to help you draw up an interesting, compelling and engaging offer for each of your segments, based on the value proposition for each one. This will help you give input into marketing communications decisions (discussed in Chapter 8). Engaging marketing communications for specific segments are not mere slogans but messages about products and services, addressing direct and indirect costs, the way they can be delivered and any promotional campaign associated with them. The degree of relationship we have with a segment already or wish to have is important in determining the tone of voice during the campaign. In addition to users and potential users, other stakeholders should be part of the engagement and marketing campaign.

Some other aspects of marketing strategy for engagement

There are several other areas of interest to marketing strategy practitioners in libraries. While developing strategy be aware of the user life cycle, the need to build loyalty within the user base (where possible), branding, managing users' experience of the service when they use it, and ensuring that the library at least meets their reasonable expectations. Make sure that the service can deliver the offers and promises you have created.

Engaging with the user life cycle

Recognise that there is a life cycle to users' relationships with the library service, so there are certain key 'touch points' to manage in different ways in order to recognise the depth of the relationship at this particular point in its development. We all expect this to be recognised in our dealings with services, public and private. How often have you been annoyed when an organisation you buy from always requests your full details every time you contact them?

In marketing management a life cycle can be applied to customers, products or brand. It has a number of stages: introduction, growth, maturity, decline and collapse. Figure 7.4 shows the life cycle of a library user.

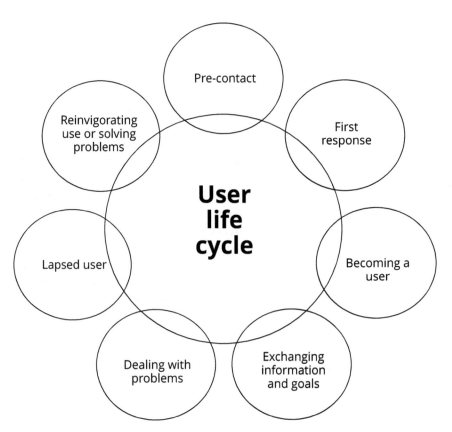

Figure 7.4 *The life cycle of a library user*

The life cycle begins before potential library users are aware of the library service. Library staff identify them and send them communications. After this first contact, potential users may make a first response, for example contact the library to see if what is offered in the communication is truly there. If this experience is positive then they become users and by the very fact of borrowing materials or using online services potentially exchange information with the library service about their use of the library. After a number of successful contacts with the library, users are likely to feel some degree of engagement or relationship with the library and its staff, and will be willing to feed back important information, which can help the library develop its offer to existing and potential new users. Library staff have the potential to build up a database of past interactions with users (e.g. on their borrowing figures, social media posts), which can be used to tailor their offers in the future. Some users may be prepared to share their personal goals publicly, and astute librarians might use their statements when thinking around service development and customisation.

For a number of reasons, some users become lapsed users, because they disengage after a problem occurs or they no longer have any reason to spend time in the library. If effort has been taken to engage with these users it may be possible to resolve problems quickly or remind them of library resources that might be of interest to them.

Building loyalty as part of an engagement strategy

One of the most important elements of an engagement marketing and customer relationship strategy is to recognise that once you have managed to attract a user to use the library it may be difficult to get that person to become a regular user, or even come in for a second time. Some marketing effort should be directed at building loyalty.

Loyalty is a difficult concept. For some private sector organisations it is measured as a user making simple repeat purchases. Others, however, managers of service organisations such as libraries, would do better to think of loyalty as an attitude a user has towards the service provider. Consider what people feel loyal towards: families, sports teams, schools, clubs, cultures, countries. People feel loyal to communities rather than organisations. Their experience of using libraries determines whether they feel engaged, part of the library community, or are simply interacting with an organisation. Loyalty can only be won if you deliver your promise well, sort out problems fast, and show a genuine commitment to helping users get what they want from the library, whether that be simply a good read or help in achieving a career aspiration. Loyalty is a potential outcome from engagement but in a busy, highly competitive world it is not easily achieved.

Engaging with the library brand

Your library brand is the set of physical attributes of your library service together with the values, beliefs and expectations surrounding it. All logos, advertising and promotional materials should be designed to evoke and emphasise these features. While you may have a style guide with guidance on colours and typefaces these are only the final outcomes from your brand identity, which is based on values and beliefs.

Use your library brand to encourage all stakeholders to engage with you. The brand should be a source of pride for your staff, and commit them to providing high-quality service. Aim for your brand to engage others through familiarity, respect and trust.

Figure 7.5 shows the objectives and outcomes of a visual rebranding for a UK public library in 2019–2020.

Public library visual rebranding

Objectives

There were two objectives in the rebranding:
- to establish a strong, clear visual brand that would stand out and differentiate the libraries from other divested organisations, charities and not-for-profit organisations; one of the challenges the libraries face is a basic lack of knowledge about its existence, and what it has achieved since 2012, even among funders and stakeholders
- to be flexible enough for staff to use across 44 sites, and across a wide range of media, including print, website and in buildings.

Outcomes

The new brand consisted of three core elements:
- a distinctive 'tab', bookmark logo, where the bottom of the text is obscured; part of the point of this was to get people examining the logo more closely, thereby helping to establish the libraries brand
- a distinctive, modern American gothic typeface (FF Good)
- a core palette of two colours, slightly modifying the purple and green the libraries had used since 2012.

Figure 7.5 *Objectives and outcomes of a visual rebranding for a UK public library in 2019–2020* (Leon Paternoster/Silk Pearce)

While many libraries use branding as a means simply to improve their physical image others have gone beyond this to truly rebrand their services and what they mean to a range of stakeholders. Tower Hamlets public library in the UK moved many years ago from describing itself by the traditional term 'library' to using the more modern term 'idea store'. Similarly York City Council (again UK) moved to present the library service under the umbrella brand 'York Explore'.

Branding or rebranding the library is not to be undertaken lightly. There are strong traditional values in the idea of libraries that many commercial organisations would be very proud to have. To move away from this in an attempt to instil new values into the idea of a library may damage the long established values. However, the world is constantly changing so it is not an option always to stand still, risking holding an archaic position in users' or other stakeholders' mindsets.

Any strategy to brand or rebrand should be considered carefully to ensure it engages rather than disengages stakeholders. When companies rebrand they often allocate significant amounts of money for such exercises, recognising that staff may well need to review the rebranding effort in five to ten years. Sometimes a product or service is right for the times and delivers as promised, as word of mouth builds the brand.

An example of the amount of work that goes into a successful rebrand can be seen from Airbnb. Their agency, Design Studio, sent four members of the agency to 13 cities. They stayed with 18 Airbnb hosts and recorded every aspect of their stay, in order to distill fully what the brand stands for. The final brand reflected the company's key values while presenting a clean, contemporary and engaging identity.

It is also possible to achieve significant engagement with your brand with what on the surface seem to be very modest products. Supreme has developed a cult following among the skateboard community. A full collection of the 253 T-shirt designs it released between 1994 and 2020 was expected to sell for US$2 million at auction with Christie's, New York, in December 2020.

If you brand or rebrand as part of your strategy ensure you employ professional help. Branding is not something the senior management team can do around the table. Also remember that whatever messages you put out as part of your branding exercise may or may not resonate with users and potential users. Brand is mainly derived from what others think about you rather than from what you decide is the way you wish to be perceived. Some say your brand is what people say about you when you leave the room.

Any branding exercise needs to affect the whole culture of the organisation to ensure the experience for all stakeholders matches the promise. For instance, branding your library as a fun organisation will be quickly undermined if frontline staff are grumpy or unhelpful. Similarly, to brand your library as a source of reliable information requires that you assess the quality of the information you relay in response to enquiries for facts rigorously.

Managing users' experience
Having looked at the value of library services to users on their terms (segmentation), created and communicated offers around this and recognised

the marketing implications of the user life cycle we need to manage users' experience by considering what we want them to feel, sense, think and do when they use the library. What will they find engaging? Are we managing the library well? Finally, how do we want the user to relate to us? Be close or distant? Is our messaging clear so we can manage user expectations well?

Table 7.4 sets out questions to think about when considering how to manage users' experience.

Table 7.4 *Managing user experience, by analysing what users feel, sense, think and do*

	What response do we want from users ?	Will they naturally make this response?	If 'yes' how can we enhance the experience? If 'no' how can we make it 'yes'?
Feel			
Sense			
Think			
Do			

Users' experience of the library is based on their interaction with communications, identity, people and systems:

- *Communications.* All your communications create an impression, either good or bad. Are they professional, setting the right tone?
- *Identity or brand.* Will the user want to be associated with you? Remember there are a number of different library user and potential user segments. Brand needs to be managed very carefully if users are to be and remain engaged.
- *People.* Your staff are a marketing asset, arguably the most important marketing asset. They deliver your offers and promises. It is no good having policy and process in place if the frontline staff present a different experience from the one promised by your marketing communications.
- *Systems and processes.* Do things work in practice as promised by your marketing message? Do users experience systems and processes in a way that is consistent with what you intend and believe is the offer? Are the processes visible and understandable by users? Is there an appropriate combination of automation and personal touch? As it takes a powerful message to woo users into the library there should be powerful controls on the process to ensure that when they come in they are not disappointed. Often it is not the first visit to the library that is important, it is encouraging them to make a second.

From a marketer's point of view there is no one perfect process. A marketing friendly process allows different approaches within an overarching system. Marketing planning and segmentation almost always reveal different ways in which users and potential users wish to engage with library services. There is no one point in the process where things will go wrong – it happens for different people at different points. Consider the stages of making a cup of tea. There are at least 15 potential steps, at each of which something could go wrong (Table 7.5). You may be able to add more.

Table 7.5 *Processes involved in making a cup of tea, and what could go wrong*

Process element	What could possibly go wrong?
1. Find out how the drinkers like their tea	Too many guest responses to remember correctly
2. Consider the environment in which it will be served	The wrong assumptions are made
3. Fill the kettle	Not enough water in for the number taking tea
4. Switch the kettle on	Insufficient pressure used so it clicks off
5. Ensure that a clean cup or mug and spoon are available	The mugs have unattractive patterns on them
6. Put milk in cup or mug	Too much or too little milk
7. Warm the teapot	Forgotten, but critical for some
8. Choose brand of tea	Your guests prefer other brands
9. Put tea or teabags in pot or cup	Wrong quantities
10. Pour boiling water into the teapot	Some spills on your fingers and burns them
11. Allow to brew	Balancing the mix of strong and weak tea is difficult for your set of guests
12. Pour tea into cup or mug	Forget to use tea strainer if tea leaves
13. Add sugar to taste	Wrong amounts dispensed
14. Stir	The plastic spoon melts a little
15. Present in the most appealing way	Some guests prefer a table cloth, which you have not provided

As things can go wrong even in the most simple processes, such as making a cup of tea, where should library marketers look for the weak links in library engagement? At what point do users and other stakeholders engage or disengage? To look for the weak links from a purely mechanical point of view is useful but not sufficient to support the engagement effort. Different segments have different views on where a process goes wrong and it is better to work from a segment point of view than an abstract view of the best possible process.

Working from a cost and economy viewpoint is acceptable given the usual economic constraints. However, be careful not to reduce stakeholders' engagement and support by creating economical processes that do not allow the service to meet their expectations. Then those stakeholders are unlikely to engage with the service.

In the example of making a cup of tea things can go wrong all through the process. For one segment the problem may be at stage 6 – not enough, or too much, milk may have been put in. For another it may be at stage 8 – the wrong brand of tea has been used. Stage 15 – presenting the tea in the most appealing way – may also prove a stumbling block. Some people prefer to drink tea out of fine quality china while others prefer a mug.

Marketing planners often deconstruct processes to identify weak points in the delivery of offers to specific segments. You too should look for critical points in key library processes that may engage or disengage stakeholders. Users' experience of the library should be smooth, well paced, efficient and enjoyable, perhaps even positively fun in some cases.

Every time a member of the library community comes into contact with your staff and service a good or a bad impression is created based on their experience of that contact – a 'moment of truth'. Your marketing communications almost certainly offer a positive experience in store for those visiting and using the library. What are your 'moments of truth' and do they contribute to user engagement or disengagement? You may be surprised at how many there are. Jan Carlzon, as President of SAS Airlines (and author of a book on moments of truth), believed his company had 50,000 moments of truth every day. That is 50,000 times a day when either a good or bad impression was made about his airline.

Recently the concept of 'moments of truth' has been developed even more. Google introduced the idea of the Zero Moment of Truth in order to reflect the modern online customer journey. This refers to when a person begins searching for information about a product or service, encountering reviews and more information about the product. While companies cannot control all online reviews, they can positively influence their online reputation through their interactions with the audience and the quality of the product. This leads to good reviews, which can encourage people to use the brand.

In library terms moments of truth are not just when someone comes into contact with the library staff but also every electronic contact from e-mail to your Twitter and Facebook posts. How many moments of truth does your library face every day and how closely do you manage them? There are likely to be many, even without factoring in the number of impressions created by people who did not interact with the staff but received impressions as they walked around the library. Users notice staff body language or typos on the website. The furniture, equipment, condition of stock, its neatness and tidiness along with the general condition of the building all make an impression. These are all engagement and marketing issues. Are you happy with how you manage moments of truth? As a marketer of library services you should aim to maximise the number of positive moments (maybe by increasing the number of positive contacts when they are identified) and fix the negative contacts, whether resulting in a complaint or not.

If you promise a positive experience to potential users in your marketing communications you are duty bound to monitor their experience. Guidance on monitoring and evaluating customer satisfaction is given in Chapter 11. Before we reach that point we need to craft some messages (Chapter 8) and choose appropriate ways to deliver them, digitally and non-digitally (Chapters 9 and 10).

At the end of this chapter you should now recognise the importance of setting priorities and creating winning offers that are more likely to engage than disengage potential users.

8

Crafting engaging messages

Once you have a deep understanding of users and their perceptions of value, a plan to manage stakeholders, and priority activities for the next planning period, it is time to craft the value proposition messages which will attract those with whom you wish to engage. This is an age where there is a fight for even the smallest amount of attention, let alone the sustained attention required to underpin true engagement. Do not rush to this stage without having worked out exactly what you are aiming for otherwise your message may be just one more message received that day and unlikely to spark interest.

Traditionally marketing messaging is built around an AIDA (attention, interest, desire and action) continuum, although there are now a number of other very similar conceptual frameworks, such as REAN (reach, engage, activate and nurture). Other approaches to this continuum are awareness–knowledge–liking–preference–conviction–purchase and awareness–intent–evaluation–trial–adoption. All these models go through a sequence of cognitive (understanding), affective (gaining attention) and behavioural (doing something) stages.

Figure 8.1 on the next page shows how the AIDA model, with learning from other models such as REAN, can be used to develop a marketing message for a library.

A set of planned marketing messages takes recipients through stages of attraction and gains their attention, to communicate something of real value to them quickly, to the point where they wish to investigate what is being offered. Finally, the messaging campaign should explain clearly how potential users can access any offer(s) made rather than simply hope recipients will find out for themselves.

Marketing messages from the library service should be well targeted and proven to be engaging to the audience they are aimed at. If they are not

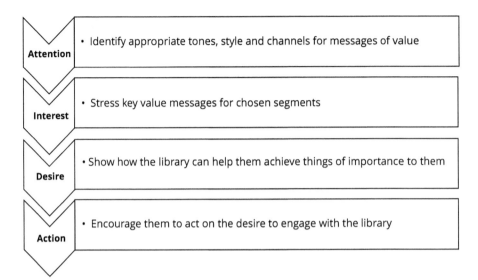

Figure 8.1 *The AIDA model used to develop a marketing message for a library*

engaging, or at least attention worthy, when potential users receive another message they may very well ignore it. Instead, if a previous message had been of interest they would pay attention to further ones. And beware, a general message sent to all stakeholders may position the library as irrelevant and recipients will pass the message by.

A strong marketing message will have within it the answers to the following questions that potential users may ask:

- What is in it for me? (See discussion of value in Chapter 5.)
- Why should I use you rather than go to another source? (This is the 'differentiator'.)
- What do you want me to do now? (The 'call to action' with relevant information – contact names, dates, times, locations and so on.)

Messages of value may be enough to get you someone's attention but they may or may not spark great interest or desire to act on the message. Engaging messages are likely to have some of the following qualities:

- *Carry some degree of emotion.* People forget what you said but never forget the way you made them feel. Ensure the message sounds or reads as if you mean and care about what you say.
- *Be unusual, perhaps include pertinent, possibly surprising, facts.* People may become intrigued by the facts and continue reading to learn more.

- *Show energy and pace*. The reader does not want to fall asleep nor lose the will to live while reading it.
- *Have visual appeal*. Remember that for many people a picture is worth a thousand words and can quickly communicate complex combinations of ideas and feelings.
- *Have personal appeal, be aimed at 'people like me'*. A major objection to some messages is that they are not aimed at 'people like me'. A great hook for a message is to present it in such a way that it clearly applies not only to a large number of people but especially to people like those to whom it has been sent.
- *Present an interesting relevant story*. Interesting and relevant stories draw us closer.
- *Offer 'free stuff', perhaps to download*. Only useful as a technique if it is truly valuable to those receiving the message. Free stuff that is not immediately valuable is simply clutter.

For marketing and engagement purposes provide evidence showing that the library can support the message's claims, which will increase its impact. If you claim that use of the library contributes to someone's goals and aspirations you must give evidence of this. To take an example: if you state that the library supports student success, how can you demonstrate this? Do library users have higher grades than students who don't use the library? How do you know? Types of evidence include quotations from students or faculty, news stories about successful people who comment on the role of the library in their success, survey results or even statistical correlations. Evidence may come from your library or elsewhere but it has to be from a source respected by those to whom you send the message.

These are some basic practicalities of crafting effective and engaging messages:

- *Be clear*. When writing or speaking to someone, be clear about your goal or message. What is your purpose in communicating with this person? If you are not sure, then your audience certainly will not be sure. Make sure that it is easy for your reader to understand your meaning.
- *Keep to the point*. Be concise.
- *Be appropriate for the chosen audience*. Do the technical terms you use fit your audience's level of education or knowledge? Are library technical terms necessary or are they simply jargon?
- *Be logical*. Make sure all points are connected and relevant to the main topic, and the tone and flow of the text is consistent.

■ *Present in a friendly, open and honest tone.* Nobody likes to read officious, boring formal copy.
■ *Be professional.* Although an engaging message should be friendly it should also show basic professionalism. Have you checked for grammatical errors? Are all names and titles spelled correctly?

Although there will be some general awareness-building messages and supporting advertising and publicity materials it is likely that more powerful messages are based around offers to specific segments. Be clear whether communications are aimed at people who already know the library or those who know little about it. Marketing communications are based around a combination of messages that inform, persuade or remind users and potential users of library services (Figure 8.2). Messages to people without any, or without a positive experience of the library, need to be informed of what the library offers. If potential users may come into the library or use services remotely, they require information about how to do so and perhaps persuasion to visit the library in person. Persuasive marketing communications are very different from those reminding existing users of services on offer. If the intended recipients of the marketing communications know the library well already, you may need to remind them what is on offer.

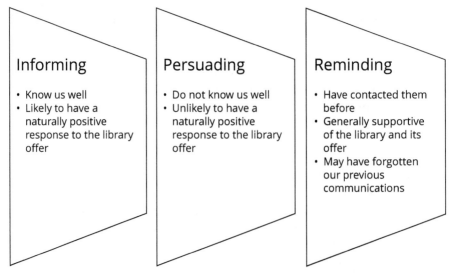

Figure 8.2 *Three types of marketing messages and the groups to which they are addressed*

Whatever combination of informing, persuading and reminding you employ in your marketing communications you should have an appropriate output. Taking a few examples from customer (user) retention and customer (potential user) acquisition strategies noted earlier, consider what the relevant approach to marketing communication should be.

One user retention strategy may be to ensure that existing local studies users do not forget that the library has a very wide range of general history books in another department, which may well add to their understanding and enjoyment of their favourite subjects. After an initial trawl for names, family historians may wish to add texture to their understanding by reading about the social background to their ancestors' lives. Marketing communications with this group could inform them of the other books on their topic. There may be an element of reminding and persuading but the general thrust will be to inform. Note that the most important question to ask with an informing marketing communication is not 'what do I want and need to tell them?' but rather 'what do *they* want to hear and need to know?'

Take another group – project teams in corporate library environments. If transactional data suggests that most users only use an expensive database infrequently this may be because they have forgotten about it. Members of the project teams might benefit from a pleasant communication reminding them about the database's existence. You could explain why it will help them with their current project. Keep aware of the development of projects within your organisation and what databases will help potential users move forward quickly and authoritatively. At the very least your reminder builds relationship and engagement with its recipients. Reminding is a more personal communication than informing and the copy for any campaign should reflect this. When trying to identify a fruitful area where users require reminders ask yourself, 'what might they have forgotten?' or even 'what might they be in danger of forgetting?' Reminding is an important marketing communication if handled sensitively and messages are not sent too frequently. No one wants to be constantly reminded of anything so only use reminders where quick wins can be expected.

For some groups strong communication techniques are required. Health service libraries may have difficulty in enlisting certain groups into library use. Although some subsets such as student nurses are natural users of library services to support their educational and research activities, others such as general practitioners may be geographically remote and under such pressure that they rarely respond to informational or reminding communications. As generalist practitioners' clinical interests are often subsumed by the pressure of managing their practices, any messages to them must be persuasive, clear and make an immediate connection. You need to explain your offer and how it could help them to achieve things of value to them. Simply informing this group about a new service is unlikely to help you to engage with them as they may not give your message enough attention to work out how your offer helps them. You need to understand each group's problems and tell them what library services would benefit them.

Having decided on your overall offer for each key segment it is time to develop a contact management strategy. The world is awash with marketing messages and many have no impact among the sea of communications. More worryingly, many consumers have a very negative attitude towards mass marketing efforts. Advertising and promotional activity can damage reputation as well as build brand.

There are two strategic options for communications to stimulate use and engagement with individual segments – push and pull strategies:

- *Push strategies* are directed towards influencers and intermediaries who can give the library access to chosen segments or who influence their feelings about, and attitudes to, the library. Marketing communications and promotions of push strategies must give an incentive to these intermediaries or influencers to encourage use of library services.
- *Pull strategies* are directed towards ultimate users and focus on creating demand from the actual user or potential user rather than through the influence of intermediaries. They are likely to take a more personal tone.

The challenge for librarians is to get messages across in a way that has an impact but is not intrusive, which requires a mix of appropriate push and pull strategies.

How often should users be contacted?

There is no mathematical formula that sets out how often users should be contacted, and indeed the right answer is not to be found in a committee sitting in a room working out the most appropriate figure.

The answer is as often as users want to be contacted. Users should be given the opportunity to tell the library how often, and when, they would like to be contacted. In marketing language this is an example of a customer managed relationship. The ideal time to gain this information is when users join the library. Those who want frequent contact should be contacted frequently; those who want no marketing messages should not receive them. There is no halfway house here that is likely to be effective and ethical.

Should library marketing communications be general or event driven?

General communications are sent to all users and potential users, and can reach a very large number of people, but might not reach users or potential users at a time when they are open or susceptible to the message being sent. Think of marketing communications you have received. Have you occasionally bought something because an inviting message came just at the right time? And how many general messages have you stored in your mind, other than as a vague impression, which you will act on in the near future?

Event-driven communications are sent at a particular time to reach users or potential users at a moment when they are likely to be interested in the subject of the message or simply when whoever sends the message believes it is appropriate for them at that time, if only they knew about it. At a very general level these are simply communications about time-specific library events, but event-driven marketing communications can be extremely sophisticated. For example, the student life cycle can be used in academic libraries to determine a series of event-driven messages that are highly appropriate at specific times of the year. Messages such as 'we know you are stressed but we're here to help you and here's how' might be particularly engaging two or three weeks before exam times.

Another useful way to think about your communication strategy is to reflect on the phrase 'speak, listen and build'. Marketing is a dialogue not simply the library broadcasting a message. For each segment remember that you have to get a conversation started and then keep it going. Anecdotal evidence suggests that some libraries often start conversations then fail to maintain the conversation over time.

When first communicating with users and potential users tell them about something that is likely to interest those with whom you are conversing. Do not only talk about your library in your marketing communications. You may be really excited that you have books and computers but recipients are likely to prefer to learn about services that are directly relevant to them. If your market research is totally divorced from your marketing communications then there is a very real danger that you will be tempted to talk about your services rather than consider what users and potential users are interested in. Give recipients information they find helpful about the library facilities and services in an engaging way.

Single marketing leaflets, radio interviews or newspaper advertisements are not enough to win the hearts and minds of stakeholders. To build a relationship with potential users library staff have to keep it going, which can lead to the library providing more successful services. For example, library staff who have a close relationship with local studies users in public libraries can tell them when there are new services, which will improve their relationship with those users.

The library has to remind users of its services. How often do you act immediately on a marketing communication that comes your way? Occasionally, but often people only respond to advertisements or messages after seeing them a number of times, whether because repeated messaging strengthens the value of the offer in their mind or because it takes them time to decide if they need the product. If this is the case why should it be different for people seeing a library message? Single marketing messages are unlikely to have a significant effect. Anyone undertaking a marketing planning process in a library should have an annual marketing communications plan addressing the reach and frequency of the advertising for different segments of library user. A wise library marketer recognises that although some users and potential users react immediately to library offers, others need to be informed and persuaded over time.

Options for a communications mix

Figure 8.3 sets out four options for communicating with users and potential users.

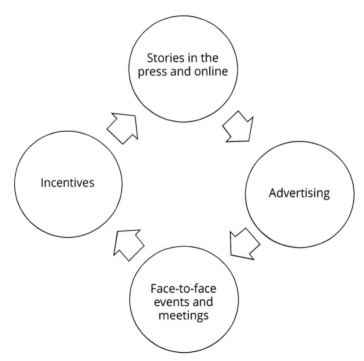

Figure 8.3 *Options for communicating with stakeholders*

The broadest form of marketing communication is creating and distributing stories about library services and events (public relations). Although this can deliver responses from day one it is best thought of as a long-term process for engagement, which underpins other communications that seek to influence immediate action directly through a compelling offer or some sort of incentive to try the service. If you have a public relations department its staff can undertake this activity, but you need to ensure their commitment long term. A library service is rarely, if ever, the most important service within its organisation and it can be difficult to maintain support for long-term activities in the face of changing departmental priorities.

Public relations personnel can be excellent in building awareness and brand but need to be supplemented to ensure that those promoting the library know how it works and can help address the needs of potential users. It may be helpful to advertise to specific segments with clear segment-specific messages, perhaps rolled out through printed materials or online communications.

Where the offer to a particular segment is complex communications may require something more powerful than printed material. Face-to-face meetings (personal selling) may be appropriate, for example, speaking directly to a specific user group, giving appropriate and targeted information so you inspire them to use the library. Personal selling is very time-consuming and should not be used merely to inform people that specific library services exist. It is perhaps the only effective way to influence funding or governance stakeholders when trying to gain their support or change their views of the library service.

There are occasions when the segments you wish to market to already know about your services and need little reminding about how they can access them. They may even be aware of the benefits of using library services, yet still they do not use them to the extent you would like. In such circumstances these potential users may need a little persuasion to use or increase their use of the library. For example, you may identify a group of modern fiction readers who you believe can be encouraged to take out more books. Perhaps they need a small incentive (a sales promotion). You could send them a message offering them a free reservation for every three reservations they pay for (assuming your library charges for reservations). You can use incentives in two ways – as a bribe to non-users to try using your library or as a reward to existing users to stimulate extra use. Anecdotal evidence from librarians who have made transactions free when they are usually paid for, such as DVD loans, as a bribe, is that this does not work especially well. Most libraries seem to be on a user acquisition trail rather than a user retention trail so it is not surprising that most uses of sales promotional methods are as bribes rather than rewards. Now the importance of user retention and engagement is recognised there is more encouragement to use sales promotion methods as rewards.

Once users become regular visitors you have to communicate with them if you wish to maintain some sort of relationship and a claim to be user centric or user driven. An important part of this communication is to monitor satisfaction levels and, crucially, respond to dissatisfaction by improving services.

Communications strategies

By now you will be aware of the need to have a general communication strategy for the library and its brand, and a segment communication strategy to ensure that you communicate directly to groups of people with similar needs and wants. The general strategy creates awareness and some degree of familiarity and comfortableness with the concept of a library and its services. The segment-specific activity allows you to sell the benefits of libraries, showing how particular types of user have benefited in the past and how others can achieve these benefits.

Consider your mix of general and segment-specific messages and note them in Table 8.1.

Table 8.1 *General and segment-specific message strategies*

General messages to all	Segment-specific messages to users, potential users and other stakeholders
1 2 3 Etc.	Segment A 1 2 3 Segment B 1 2 3 Segment C 1 2 3 Etc.

It is very unlikely that you can undertake the full set of marketing communications you have identified. All libraries have limited, often very limited, resources for their communication strategy and there is a tendency to look for activities which do many things at once. While one should always be alert to this possibility there is a danger of trying to communicate too many messages to too many people through one campaign.

If you find yourself deciding marketing activity in a committee, beware of the tendency for 'group think'. This will almost certainly compromise the power of your potential messages. Remember that users are looking for things that help them achieve things of value to them, not what members of funding bodies might think that they are funding libraries for.

Once the set of communications in general and by segment has been chosen then a number of key questions arise:

- What shall we say?
- How shall we say it?
- What should they think?
- What should they do?

Underpinning this thinking is the previously introduced concept of AIDA – a flow of outcomes from our communications from grabbing their Attention, developing their Interest, awakening their Desire to use the library, resulting in their Action to use the library.

For each communication be aware which part of AIDA is being addressed. Each requires different content (what shall we say?) and tone (how shall we say it?). Over a year you might send a target segment a series of messages that takes them along this path. While it is not impossible to take a person from unawareness to action with one campaign, this is not easy and requires an overwhelmingly compelling offer, highly tailored to that person's needs so they instinctively see the benefits of the offer to them and are willing and able to make the immediate effort to do something about it. When thought of in such terms it becomes clear that in most cases users need to be exposed to a series of messages before any action on their part can be expected. Sending out a leaflet on a Wednesday and then timetabling extra staff to cope with the influx on Saturday is unlikely to be a successful marketing communications strategy.

When creating marketing communications there are many factors to consider. For each intended communication give some thought to:

- *Why?* What are you trying to achieve with this communication? Is it realistic and achievable? Have you been overconfident in your assessment of probable impact?
- *Who?* Have you clearly targeted who is to receive this message?
- *What?* Is the message you intend to communicate clear in your mind?
- *Where?* Do you know which media you are going to use? Direct mail? Radio? In-library display? Social media?
- *How?* Will the message be based on text or pictures? Will the tone be serious or humorous? Will it be general or be based on testimonials from other readers who have received the benefits your message will communicate?

- *When?* When is the appropriate time of year to run each message? How many times should the message be delivered per year?
- *How much?* Are the costs of the communications clear?
- *Schedule?* Have you planned the activity over a one-year integrated planning framework to ensure the weight of advertising required to have significant impact?
- *Response?* Have you considered the potential responses and how to deal with them? For instance if new users are to be encouraged does the library have the necessary welcome packs and any supporting relationship marketing materials?
- *Evaluation?* All of this activity will have involved significant staff effort and have incurred direct costs too. Are costs in time and money being monitored to enable the calculation of some degree of return on marketing investment? Marketing communications should not simply be an act of faith.

As funds for marketing are inevitably limited in most library authorities, try to identify marketing communications activities which can have a long-lasting impact or ability to create some degree of awareness over time. There may even be opportunities to leverage marketing activities.

As an example, a library event may be an excellent way to show the community how important the library is in the life of the area, organisation or company. An excellent event attended by 50 people will create much goodwill and the right thoughts in those who attended. However, in our example, only 50 people attended, even though the event had been widely publicised. How can this be leveraged? Well, organisers can hope that these 50 people will tell their friends how good an event this was. Such influencer marketing is proving very effective in these times of an over production of marketing messages.

Think of ways to encourage readers to talk among themselves about the library. Some of the greatest marketing successes of our times have been built on a first class product surrounded by viral marketing buzz. To prove the point consider what you think is the best search engine. Some say it depends on what you want to do, but the most popular view is likely to be Google. And how much advertising have you seen from Google? A relatively small amount. Nevertheless the buzz around Google has been excellent word-of-mouth marketing.

These are some forms of marketing communications:

- annual reports
- articles in the press and local magazines

- banners on websites and buildings to publicise library events
- billboards and outside poster advertising
- bookmarks as a simple reminder
- brochures to convey the atmosphere in a library
- bus advertising to get good geographical coverage
- car park tickets with printed advertisements or promotions
- celebrity endorsements of the value of the library
- classified advertisements in telephone and other directories as a source of reference to users
- competitions to introduce the fun elements into your communications
- direct mail to target your message
- displays to show your wares
- editorials that position the importance of the library
- e-mail to develop relationships with users
- events to put energy and movement into the library offer
- exhibitions
- inserts with payslips of local authority staff as an example of targeted communications
- leaflets about service
- letters to the editor to show library viewpoints
- networking to keep alert to changing user needs and opportunities to serve
- newsletters to provide an ongoing dialogue with users
- newspaper advertisements to publicise events
- 'outreach' visits by staff
- postcards as a way to reinforce a more general message
- posters displayed in library
- posters displayed in non-library premises (e.g. leisure facilities, adult education centres, shopping centres, health centres, buses, railway stations)
- press releases to manage a relationship with the press
- public service announcements on radio as a general communication
- public speaking to inspire library use
- publishing to show expertise
- radio advertisements as a general communication and brand building
- signs to direct and emphasise
- stands at shows and fairs to have library presence at key community events
- telemarketing to help widen library reach or develop relationships with existing users
- television advertisements are expensive and unlikely but where negotiated can offer an opportunity to show the creativity of the library

- user testimonials to show evidence of value
- videos of past library events to show energy
- visits to schools, playgroups, colleges, local organisations, community groups, business organisations
- website to inform, remind and inspire
- welcome pack to create a good first impression
- word of mouth to generate buzz.

It is appropriate to use a combination of many of these forms of marketing and other options under a single integrating banner or campaign. The Public Library Association in the USA ran a campaign called 'The Smartest Card', which integrated posters, toolkits, celebrity endorsement and news releases. Local libraries produce specific brochures and attend local events to communicate their message. A combination of approaches is appropriate to convey the message that of all the cards in your target users' wallets the library card is the most valuable.

The return on marketing communications investment

There are clearly many potential marketing options for libraries. Decide which combination of approaches is best to meet the marketing objectives by thinking about the return you will get for your marketing spend. Although some marketing is undertaken for general brand building it is not wise to think of marketing as an act of faith. Like all library activities there are costs associated with marketing and where money or effort is spent you should attempt to show a good return.

There are three important concepts to help judge the most economical way to achieve your marketing objectives:

- *Reach*. Calculate the number of different target or potential users who are exposed to a message at least once during a specific period of time.
- *Frequency*. Calculate the number of times an individual is exposed to a given message during a specific period of time.
- *Cost per contact*. From reach, frequency and the cost of the communication it is possible to calculate the cost of reaching one member of the target market. This is a useful benchmark figure to use for subsequent planning rounds.

If these key marketing measurement concepts are kept firmly in mind there is every chance that you can make good decisions on the type of approaches to take in your marketing communication efforts.

You need to be effective as well as economical and efficient. Indeed, being efficient and economical but totally ineffective is not a good use of time or money even if the reach, frequency and cost per contact figures are impressive. The expected outcome of any marketing activity is that users, potential users and other stakeholders will do more of what you wanted them to do when you started to think about your marketing. If they do not then no inter-authority comparisons on marketing costs can have any impact except in the political arena. The political arena is very important to the future funding of public library services but remember that the interests of users and politicians are not always the same.

Do users and potential users respond to library communications?

You can lead a horse to water but you can't make it drink. Remember this. Your marketing activity can inform, remind and even persuade but users and potential users may object to your message and you may not be close enough to them to recognise this. Often the main barrier to surmount is apathy, though if you have undertaken the value analysis suggested earlier in this book then it is to be hoped that apathy will not be a significant hurdle – you will provide something of value to potential users now, not something that is vaguely interesting to them at some point in the future.

Assuming that you have created a good marketing strategy based on achieving specific marketing objectives, turned that strategy into a series of well-chosen activities over a year and assessed the likely reach, frequency and cost per contact, temper any temptation to sit back and breathe a sigh of relief with a nagging worry – it seems OK in theory but what will happen in practice?

Even if the marketing strategy is executed well and all the activities you promise take place on time and in full you may still encounter barriers in messaging. These are some of the sceptical or negative comments that potential users may make:

- *'I don't believe you.'* Before you run your campaign be honest with yourself. Is the communication about something that the library can realistically deliver? Will the users or potential users have different experiences of the library than those advertised in the publicity and promotions? Put bluntly, will they believe that the library can deliver its promise?
- *'I don't need it.'* Is the library offering things which users and potential users perceive to be of value? Do they really need it? Are we acting as social engineers telling them that they need it?

- *'I don't have enough time.'* When they read or see library publicity are users and potential users likely to reject the offer because it is not convenient for them to take it up? Have we communicated not just that whatever is being offered is valuable in helping users in their work or projects but also that it is easily accessed in ways that are convenient to them?
- *'I don't have enough money.'* Has the message of the true cost of library service been communicated? Public librarians are still often amazed at the number of new or potential users who expect the library to charge for a service. Do marketing messages set out how much users are expected to pay for a service? Remember that some users may not be able to afford the cost of travelling to the library. Has this potentially hidden cost been considered when creating marketing communications?
- *'It won't work for me.'* Is there any evidence in the publicity that whatever you are offering will work for any particular user? Nothing communicates the benefit of using a service in a message faster than seeing a testimonial that promotes its value. Learning from Chapter 5 on the importance of segmentation it is clear that if only general library benefits are advertised in publicity material there is the distinct possibility that recipients will ignore it.
- *'Zzzzzzzz.'* Sometimes the library message is so boring and dry that the receiver is more likely to fall asleep than pay attention to what you are saying.

If your current messages and promotions cannot address the six basic objections set out above then do not expect users to engage with your library service. Remember that although there may be good answers to these objections, if they are not managed as part of the marketing campaign potential users may never come close enough to the library for library staff to have an opportunity to discuss their objections. It is very dangerous to assume that the library simply needs to inform users and potential users of library services and as a consequence those users will immediately understand the benefits of using the library.

Table 8.2 opposite shows some possible responses to sceptical or negative comments potential users of the library might make on receiving library publicity.

Marketing communications at different stages of the user life cycle

There are specific marketing and communications activities to be used at each stage of the user life cycle (introduced in Chapter 7).

Table 8.2 *Responses that could be made to sceptical or negative comments about library publicity*

Objection to engagement	Response from library staff
'I don't believe you'	'We have evidence to show our promises are delivered'
'I don't need it'	'Our research shows beyond doubt that people like you do need it and they need it now'
'I don't have enough time'	'We have outlined a quick way to access what you need'
'I can't afford it'	'The cost of the service is clearly stated and free services are highlighted in bold'
'It won't work for me'	'Please read the testimonials from people like you who have the same immediate needs; they have used the service successfully and found it valuable'
'Zzzzz'	'Our research suggests you could find it helpful to use the library'. Ensure the language and tone of the communication is appropriate to this type of user. Presentation can, in some circumstances, be more engaging than content

Pre-contact

At this early stage in the user life cycle the important marketing activities are targeting, segmentation (based on an understanding of users' needs, wants and the value that the library service can bring them) and lifetime value calculations. Marketing messages should reflect the diversity of potential users and stakeholders rather than provide a single message. At this point they know little about the library and you know little about them. However, your pre-targeting research should have given you enough knowledge to add a degree of customisation to your marketing messages to this group.

First response

When potential users respond to first marketing messages an effective enquiry management process or system should be in place with supporting standards of response. This is a very early stage of engagement and potential new users quickly form an opinion about your service. You never get a second chance to form a first impression.

Becoming a user

Once potential users make their first tentative step to visit the library or log in to its online products there is an opportunity to get the relationship off to a good start by having appropriate welcoming procedures. Library staff who have attempted to find out a little about new users could offer a highly individual welcome pack. If done with sincerity this could encourage engagement.

Exchanging information

As users continue to access library services they leave a trail of transactions, which can be used in a marketing context to help library staff understand how individuals use the library. This data-driven approach should underpin all specific marketing communications. For trust to develop (which is essential for engagement), use this data clearly for the benefit of users and meet their privacy concerns with robust data protection policies.

Exchanging goals

As the relationship between library and user develops the positive atmosphere encourages deeper trust and engagement. Users may well trust you more and more with information about themselves and what their life goals are if they have good experiences of the library and therefore trust you to use their personal data responsibly. Some will allow you to use this data to tailor the service to them because they believe it is safe with you and you will use it responsibly to their benefit. This is less likely to be possible with very new users as a climate of trust will not have developed yet. Marketing messages to new users should address their likely needs rather than simply respond to explicit requests for service.

Dealing with problems

Even in the most efficient of libraries, there are times when users feel that the service given is not what they would expect, and there is potential to lose them. Those responsible for marketing should be aware of users at risk and manage potential disengagement accordingly, for example through complaint handling procedures. Marketing messages should not over-promise and under deliver.

Loss and recovery

Good marketers do not simply shrug their shoulders as users desert their libraries. Put in place procedures for finding out why users stop using the library and attempt to re-engage them through marketing communications and campaigns. Human contact via the telephone is likely to be most persuasive, as it is personal, and a significantly more effective marketing communication than e-mail or another approach.

Event-driven and segment-specific marketing communications messages

As noted earlier, marketing communication messages for engagement can be either general or segment specific and long lasting (over an extended period) or event driven (for a specific event) (Table 8.3). General long-lasting messages are very useful for establishing brand values and are a support to more engaging event-driven messages.

We look at each of these four categories in turn.

Table 8.3 *Examples of general and segment-specific long-lasting and event-driven messages*

	General messages to all	Segment-specific messages
Key long-lasting messages	Library as source of trusted information Library as inspiration Library as haven Library as source of corporate value creation Library as a source of health information	Children grow emotionally through reading Access to library service for remote users
Event-specific messages	Halloween fun Annual reading week events Help for students at exam time Inspiration at student induction Opening of new library	Meeting for local historians New subscription to database for cardiology

Long-lasting messages with general interest

General messages position the library as a source of value related to the practical application of its vision, mission and values, for example:

Libraries help communities thrive

Librarians – the ultimate search engines

Change your life with books

Libraries – the door to the world

Cutting libraries in a recession is like cutting hospitals in a plague

Discover. Connect. Inspire

If you want to get laid, go to college. If you want an education, go to the library.

The messages tend to be broad reminders of the value of libraries, and are often slogans, which grab users' attention and have the potential to position the library in the user or potential user's mind in some engaging way.

Sometimes slogans can underpin a sustained marketing campaign over several years. In the USA, for instance, the Public Library Association committed itself to the Campaign for America's Libraries by adopting the slogan, 'Smartest Card. Get it @your library' with a three-year programme to make the library card 'the most valuable card in your wallet'. This is an engaging slogan that can be used frequently as an attention grabber, even if it is not of itself sufficiently targeted to have a direct impact on habits. Such slogans can provide an umbrella for more targeted campaigns.

Make sure to test slogans before distributing them widely through a number of marketing channels. Not everyone finds slogans engaging and some are positively disengaged by what others find attractive.

Consider using fact sheets, press releases, a contact list for the media and case studies of how the library has made a difference to people's lives. Do you have a media kit to send on demand to the local newspaper or radio station? You could make it available via your website as journalists are often pushed by deadlines. If they have quick access to information it can make the difference between them mentioning and not mentioning the library in a story. See Chapter 9 for discussion on the media.

Long-lasting messages with segment-specific messages

Long-lasting messages to distinct segments of library users outline the value of particular products and services to them. For example, a general leaflet for 'silver surfers' (older people learning the internet) may be produced and used in occasional campaigns. It will have the same information about how to access the internet as messages for other groups, but unlike them stress that recipients should not hesitate to ask for help should they need it.

Event-specific messages for general use

Event-specific messages for general use are useful for general brand building but unlikely to inspire immediate library use. Events are gatherings for specific purposes: a book club in a public library; a general open coffee session to 'get to know the library' in a corporate library; a demonstration of a new online database subscription in an academic or health service library. Messages promoting events give information on key details relating to the event, such as when and where it takes place, and may cover the benefits of using the library, but are not specific enough to appeal to general library users. They may have a different layout and design from library publications addressed to a wide range of users.

Event-specific messages for particular segments

Events for specific segments are more specific than those held for library users in general, for example subject-specific classes, programmes or lectures, and sub-categories of user such as teenagers, part-time students or jobseekers might benefit from specifically targeted communications. Such messages should address the characteristics of the event or segment within the context of the group involved. For example, in public libraries there may be messages promoting materials for teenagers, young mothers or jobseekers. In academic libraries messages might be directed to part-time students who live far away from the library buildings but would greatly benefit from using its online resources from home.

Media kits

Ensure that at all times you have a set of marketing messages and communications that is ready for a range of applications. When a radio or newspaper journalist requests material, library staff should be able to respond quickly and efficiently. You should know how you will respond to approaches from the media. Are there real, engaging human stories in library publicity material, for example? A press release or stock story with details of how an individual used the library and benefited from it greatly (in their terms!) is far more attractive to the media than a finely crafted informational leaflet. The media want their readers, listeners and viewers to be engaged so the library should have interesting stories to tell if it expects to receive positive media attention.

A good marketer is proactive and finds opportunities to engage with the media. Appoint a dedicated spokesperson who not only responds to queries but also identifies stories suitable to bring to the attention of media representatives. Libraries should make news through interesting and engaging stories that involve human interactions with the library. A good library marketer not only identifies contacts in the local media but has a good idea of the sort of stories each contact has been involved with in the past and what they are currently looking for.

Cast your mind back to when you last read your local newspaper. What attracted you most? For many of us it was either joyous or sad stories of people's lives rather than the business stories of the new machinery installed at the local postal sorting office. There are many joyous stories relating to public libraries in particular that are not currently promoted. They enhance the library's importance to its local community. Here are some examples:

By using the library Eric found fellow railway enthusiasts and before long was enjoying volunteering on a local heritage railway.

Consulting an antiques guide in the library, Ynez found she had a very exciting and valuable item. She sold it and then went on a once in a lifetime voyage around the world.

Chuck became a sound engineer after being inspired by the rock band that played at a library event. Then he read all the relevant books in the library and more provided by interlibrary loans.

The character of engaging marketing is not a simple leaflet outlining the number of books and computers on offer or the opening hours. Communicate inspiration rather than simply information and the library is well on the way to engaging its user community and key stakeholders.

Create a media kit if you do not have one already. It will be a useful resource and force you to think about your library's role in the local community. Be prepared with library success stories in case a journalist approaches you one hour before their copy deadline. This could encourage them to engage with you again when they remember that you offered a great story when they were under pressure.

In the media kit include brochures, fact sheets, photographs, a key contacts list of staff who can act as spokespersons on specific topics, copies of logos or other graphic material to help with library branding, case studies and some general quotes attributable to individuals in the library. Most importantly, review the media kit annually as part of the marketing planning process: out of date contacts and quotes will do more harm than good.

Writing copy for marketing communications

Librarians are not taught copywriting skills as part of their professional education, but many are in the position of being accidental marketers as marketing in libraries is only occasionally supported by sufficient funds to employ professional copywriting consultants. Public relations and media relations departments sometimes have skills in-house, but access to such expertise by library staff is often limited as these professionals work with parts of the organisation that are deemed more important.

In such circumstances library staff should be aware of some basic practical principles of writing effective copy: it should be relevant (to those at whom it is aimed), original and impactful. When writing copy:

- *Make sure you are succinct and keep focus.* Every word should matter. It is possible to offer too much information. Be aware of what you are trying to do and do not try to do too many things at once in your marketing communication.
- *Try to be very specific.* Address your segment of interest and not some idea of a general reader. There is no such general reader.
- *Get personal.* If your copy has 'human interest' it is more likely to be engaging. A good way to include a personal dimension is to try to include real testimonials. Your copy should not only claim benefits for your service but show how real people have received those benefits from the library and recognise them as benefits.
- *Try to look for an original angle.* Look for an unexpected twist or association, a play on words or a catchy phrase. Analogies and metaphors can add interest to a message. Beware of devising over-clever slogans that have little or no content when challenged but sound good around the senior management table.
- *Use the language of conversation.* Many marketing communications aim to encourage action from whoever is reading them, whether user, potential user or other stakeholder. If you do not make this clear why will stakeholders bother to respond to library messages?

There are various message formats:

- *straightforward*: based on an informational message
- *demonstration*: describes how to use the service
- *comparison*: shows how the library is the best place to undertake particular research or other activity, or to solve a problem; for example, the library might be seen as the solution to a search for suppliers of a specific product
- *endorsement*: useful if you have celebrities to help build credibility
- *'teaser'*: where the library is not identified but implied.

Promotional activity

Having created a set of engaging marketing messages to help you inform, persuade or remind your users, potential users and other stakeholders of your services, it is nearly time to choose the channels to deliver and amplify them.

Consider first if your messages are strong and engaging enough for recipients to read them and know how to respond, if required. You may consider using special promotions to attract people to use your services if those services are not in themselves sufficiently attractive. Promotions can be used as either 'bribes' (e.g. to non-users to try the library) or 'rewards' (e.g. to thank users for their patronage and encourage even more use).

Here are two examples of a promotion used as a 'bribe':

■ The New York Public Library (NYPL) has a library shop (www.thelibraryshop.org), which includes a whole range of materials for sale. However, it is very much tied in with NYPL's activities and a bookmark notes, 'Become a member of the New York Public Library today and receive a 10% discount on all your purchases at The Library Shop.'
■ Registering for the Children's Summer Reading Programme in Dunedin Library (New Zealand) entitles the person who registers to a free video or DVD voucher.

Here are two examples of a promotion used as a 'reward':

■ Portsmouth City Libraries (UK) offer a reward for joining the library: 'Your card gives you free access to the internet and Microsoft Office on our library computers, and the following discounts in the city: 20% off Full Navy Tickets to Portsmouth Historic Dockyard; 20% discount with Hovertravel; 20% discount at Mozzarella Joe's Pizza Restaurant (up to eight people per table and not valid in conjunction with any other offers); £2 off standard admission to the Blue Reef Aquarium; 10% discount at Blossoms of Portsmouth, florist; free swimming at selected Portsmouth pools for those aged 12 and under.'
■ Lisle Library District (25 miles west of Chicago, USA) offers points and local discounts. Each physical item checked out is worth 10 points, and users can earn a maximum of 100 points per week. Points never expire and can be redeemed for goods at local businesses.

Less exciting promotional offers that may be worth considering are giving away free badges, notepads, pens, balloons, frisbees and a host of other items suitably embellished with appropriate logos and graphics. More useful in some places might be the offer of free car parking time for library users. Library suppliers and national organisations (e.g. www.literacytrust.org.uk) often have downloadable printed promotional materials. Some regional public libraries (e.g. Alberta Libraries; www.visityourlibrary.net) also have free promotional and advertising materials to browse online and download. Although often specific to individual library authorities, they are a good source of ideas for your own promotional messages and supporting activity.

It is often possible to align libraries with initiatives such as a national reading day or bid for funding from programmes such as the Carnegie Trust led Engaging Libraries programme. The 18-month Phase 2 supports public libraries across the UK to deliver public engagement projects on research into health, society and culture.

Through alignment with such programmes libraries receive some degree of funding together with professional help and support, and sometimes centrally produced marketing communications and promotional activity. However, it is possible to over-emphasise support for national initiatives at the expense of undertaking deep, highly specific, marketing communications and promotions with your local users and potential users. Will they engage with national or local initiatives?

Complete the marketing communications with a set of internal communications to ensure all staff understand the messages sent out and the expected range of responses they need to deal with. Internal communication methods include face-to-face discussion, newsletters, letters, notes, memos, posters on notice boards and e-mail. Do not forget to tailor messages to each stakeholder group. Remember that you have to inspire staff to support the ideas behind the marketing communications, particularly to users and potential users. Simply informing staff of the communications sent out is not enough.

Now you have an engagement strategy (Chapter 7) and a marketing communications programme (this chapter) attention turns to identifying and deciding on the appropriate mix of channels to distribute library messages.

9

Effective marketing channels for engaging messages

Now that you have developed powerful, engaging, attention-worthy messages for those you wish to engage with it is time to decide how to deliver and amplify the message. There are many channels through which messages can be spread and not all are appropriate for all communications and user groups. Different channels suit different audiences and may need to be adapted for specific groups.

Be aware that users and other stakeholders receive messages from you even if you are unaware that you are sending them. For example, the physical condition and layout of your buildings either attracts or repels potential visitors. Compare an airy, bright, colourful and exciting children's area of a school library placed at the centre of the school with a grey-walled, small, windowless library hidden away off the main corridor in another school. It is difficult to be engaging with the unattractive. What implicit messages is your physical library or online presence saying about the service? Furthermore, if the staff don't deliver the library promises made through the library's messaging their behaviour is likely to derail potential engagement. Perhaps worse, even if the library is delivering its promises but only slowly, by a surly, unfriendly, discourteous staff, this may constrain significant engagement regardless of the quality of your stock or buildings.

Promotional library messages can be delivered by:

- word of mouth
- champions
- profiles of users
- events and presentations, training sessions, talks
- outreach and advocacy activities
- telephone conversations.

Interactive non-digital approaches may be used:

- reading campaigns
- competitions and quizzes within the library.

These are some traditional media used to promote library messages:

- radio, TV, press local and national, professional journals
- print advertisements
- leaflet drops
- posters
- brochures
- annual report
- magazine articles
- newsletters.

Messages can be promoted within libraries physically and digitally, using:

- display
- signs
- buttons and badges
- library guides
- profiles of library staff
- library tours
- messages on promotional items such as pens and bookmarks
- kiosks
- social media posts
- website
- apps
- blogs
- podcasts
- e-mail
- video.

Digital channels are very important for many user groups but care needs to be taken when using them to deliver messages as they have some disadvantages over traditional channels. Two-way conversations and interactivity are very useful and potentially engaging, but disengaged users or other stakeholders can easily and quickly destroy your reputation via digital channels unless you are constantly aware of the online conversations where damage can be done. Complaints, whether justified or not, can be amplified across your follower base when made digitally. Digital channels and engagement is discussed in Chapter 10.

We turn now to look at non-digital methods of marketing messages and their ability to be engaging while also credible, authoritative and interesting.

Non-digital methods of marketing messages
People and conversation

Library staff are potentially the most powerful channel for communicating engaging messages if they enthusiastically promote library messages and are well aware of the needs and wants of potential users. They should embody the library's values – be friendly, helpful, outgoing, expert, intelligent, approachable, reliable and highly visible. All these characteristics are endearing and engaging. Many other messaging channels are unable to replicate these characteristics.

Perhaps the most impressive channel for such an approach is 'word of mouth' or referral marketing. Consumers are rightly aware of the limitations of product descriptions made by the suppliers of products or services, especially when buying a service where it matters who performs it. Libraries, being a service rather than a simple product, have potentially much to gain through word-of-mouth communication.

The response to any library claim through traditional impersonal channels may well be 'they would say that wouldn't they'. Consumers have, perhaps rightly, become cynical about traditional marketing. Much more credible and engaging is a referral from a friend, relation or colleague. For example, if you are looking for a plumber you may be hesitant to choose one from a directory or a leaflet pushed through your door because it is not always easy to judge the quality of the tradesperson if you haven't used them before. Friends and colleagues who have used the services of a plumber in the past can make recommendations or warn you of potential poor tradesmen and guide you to the better professionals. You need to be confident that if asked for a source of information a friend would recommend the library as the first call.

Many people would prefer a recommendation from a friend, relation or colleague because they trust their judgement. This is powerful marketing – having people who would recommend you to their friends. Sometimes your friends tell you about great service they have received even if you haven't asked them about it. For instance, the great restaurant service and food they had last night, the brilliance of the film on television last night, or how good their new phone is compared with their last one.

Given its importance, how can this referral through word-of-mouth marketing be developed as a channel to ensure that your messages are engaging? Here are some ways to encourage 'word of mouth':

- Make sure your library service and its offers are of high quality, that you deliver as promised and whenever possible it exceeds expectations. You definitely do not want negative word-of-mouth comments to be passed on as they are very difficult to counter, not least because you may not even know about them.
- Innovate by being different (in a useful way) to become a topic of conversation. Through previous research you should have identified some real unmet needs in your library population which even users, potential users or other stakeholders cannot fully articulate. Introduce new, powerful services and approaches and you will be seen as thought leaders – always an engaging characteristic.
- Use testimonials and endorsements from users and other engaged stakeholders in your printed and digital communications. Encourage referral and 'tell a friend' type approaches.
- Organise events and discussion groups, creating an infrastructure for people to talk to each other. Make sure these events work well for those attending and you truly do deliver your promises. You do not want negative comments. Be seen as professionals rather than amateurs simply 'having a go'.

Library champions

Another way to encourage face-to-face engaging transmission of the library message is to create library champions. This is particularly popular as an engagement strategy in academic libraries but can have applications in all types of libraries. Library champions are student volunteers who act as advocates for the library to students and staff. They often collate feedback and suggestions from fellow students on how the library services can be improved. Working on the principle that we trust the opinions of 'people like us' it is natural to have students advocating libraries to students. Library champions need to be trained in the role so they have detailed knowledge of the library services on offer and feedback techniques. They should be willing to commit an agreed number of hours per academic year. A delicate balance of commitment and passion needs to be struck as students should not feel that their role as a library champion takes up too much of their time but still take their responsibility seriously.

Library champions can be found in public libraries. For example in British Columbia, Canada, the Library Champions Project is a rolling three-month volunteer programme for new immigrants. Library champions are trained to conduct outreach to other new immigrants. The project's four training sessions focus on building communication, presentation and outreach skills and on the range of programmes, services and resources that are available in libraries and the community. After being trained, library champions develop a three-month realistic outreach plan, sharing information with friends, family, colleagues and individual community members; giving group presentations; speaking with community agencies; and using social media to inform and build relationships. Project facilitators from the library service support the champions with their outreach by helping them identify additional contacts and overcoming any challenges that they might encounter. On average, each library champion shares information with more than 50 other new immigrants. As of April 2020, close to 1,500 new immigrants had been trained as library champions and these individuals had reached out to about 85,000 other new immigrants.

Whether students advocating library services to other students in academic libraries or new immigrants reaching out to other new immigrants in public libraries, it is likely that there is much potential for these champions engaging with potential users of library services. Library champions are likely to understand these potential users' needs and be more likely to win their attention than librarians are, as they are seen as authority figures. Champions should have an outgoing character, be approachable, friendly and have a good knowledge of the library service and the benefits it can bring people like them.

Representative user profiles

Not all library supporters want to become involved in a formal or semi-formal relationship to promote the library but often they are prepared to lend their support in less formal ways. There is the opportunity to develop profiles of representative real users who have positive things to say about the library. These profiles can then, with permission, be used in your print and digital marketing at appropriate points in specific campaigns. They should include engaging detail and go beyond what might be included in any personas created for market segmentation.

Events and presentations, training sessions, talks, story telling

Events and presentations can be excellent showcases for the library and its offer, either explicitly (e.g. open days) or implicitly (e.g. being promoted by someone who supports the library message). If a presentation is engaging then attendees are likely to be interested in your communications about future events, bring their friends and experience those good feelings again.

The first element in creating an engaging event or presentation is to ask what anyone would gain by attending it and then to consider the setting. It is no good having the best speaker on the most interesting topic if the background atmosphere is uncomfortable and unattractive. If you are charging for an event, make sure it is easy to pay (perhaps by using Eventbrite or similar) and the payment process is smooth. Library users will remember if they have difficulty signing up to attend. It is best practice to create specific apps for each event giving administrative information and allowing for, and actively encouraging, online blogging or tweeting while it takes place. It is worth looking for opportunities for live polling, quizzes and other engaging activities during events.

When hosting an event or presentation, make sure it is surrounded by a positive ambience. You might try to engage the interest of those attending through live blogging, tweeting or broadcasting posts onto a large screen in the venue (e.g. via Everwall) or via livestreams through Facebook Live or YouTube. There is more on using digital channels for engagement in Chapter 10.

Retain the attention of those attending any event or presentation through interaction, collaboration and stimulation. One person talking for an hour is often boring. Choose shorter, quicker sessions wherever you can.

While innovative use of technology can be a powerful way to involve attendees at library events and presentations, one of the most powerful engagement tools is the element of surprise – providing something more and better than expected. Unexpected incidents create the most memorable moments for attendees and can result in potentially positive discussions. These may not be as easy to accomplish during library-based events as they are in other sectors (e.g. concerts can build in surprise with unscheduled guest appearances by famous musicians). However, if you are creative you might think of some way to surprise and delight a library audience. Why not have pop-up performances for instance? Announce in the library that in 30 minutes time a certain event will take place in part of the library.

While these events may not attract very large numbers it is highly likely that, if appreciated and well targeted, these events are memorable. Hold them a number of times and you may develop a reputation for innovation and excitement. This may work well in academic libraries. For instance, during exam time when students are suffering 'burn out', studying at library desks long into the night, why not have a ten-minute disco at midnight, announced at 11.45pm, to throw some energy into the ring to prevent the potential tedium of sustained revision?

Think beyond your existing financial resources as you may be able to recruit partners to deliver part of the experience you seek to provide. There may be scope to find sponsorship for the more demanding ideas and negotiating support with new stakeholders may well turn into an excellent engagement activity in itself for the library.

With any event there are pre-event, during event and post-event opportunities to develop engagement, for example, after the event:

- Publish content from the event. For example, send the link of any livestream you recorded to those who attended so they can watch it again if they wish.
- Suggest attendees sign up to your social media accounts.
- Use the event content for other purposes. If you undertook surveys or quizzes during the event you could use them as infographics to give a snapshot of what attendees thought. Later you could use them discreetly as part of your marketing collateral for future events and promotions.
- Keep the conversation going through surveys and polls.
- Reflect on the characteristics of attendees and identify why it is in their interest to keep the conversation open with you and with each other.

Outreach and advocacy activities

Outreach activities tend to raise awareness of potential users in the short to medium term. Advocacy activities tend to be medium- to long-term plans focused on other stakeholders, especially those who are sources, or potential sources, of funds, or who can influence the political climate in favour of libraries in a locality or organisation.

Events and group presentations can be part of outreach and advocacy activities but the most effective outreach and advocacy is likely to be through engaging personal meetings supported by materials and events. Outreach and advocacy have a challenging objective – to influence the way stakeholders feel about the library and their relationship to it. This is unlikely to be accomplished simply in an e-mail or poster, or a seeming good value event with a large audience potential, unless your objective is simply to develop awareness of the library through very basic outreach. Certainly if your objective is to deliver a successful change of view or relationship via advocacy then you require a complex message stated crisply to chosen stakeholders over a period of time. Engagement is not easily achieved.

These are some tips for creating engaging and successful outreach and advocacy:

- Spend plenty of pre-activity time understanding who you are trying to engage with. Go into the activity with a clear idea of who you need to influence, why, and why you are likely to be successful with your efforts. Do not try to be everything to everyone, as too broad a message is unlikely to resonate with your users through outreach, or your financial and political influencers through advocacy. Everyone is driven by their own agendas. Fit into them or prepare to be irrelevant.
- Rally your already engaged users and stakeholders and consider how you can use them to support your new efforts and give you access to those you wish to approach. It is difficult to undertake outreach or advocacy activities alone.
- After this reflection it is time to design a programme. Outreach may take place over a short to medium period with relatively quick returns. For example, in an academic library, outreach to postgraduate masters students can only take place in their early university days if they are to gain the benefits of your programme before they leave the university. However, an advocacy programme in a corporate library setting can continue over years if you need several rounds of discussion with decision-makers within the organisation.
- When you have devised your programme consider undertaking a risk assessment of what might go wrong and how you would deal with this. Advocacy, and even in some cases outreach, can be a high risk activity with the opportunity to disengage as well as engage those you seek to influence. What would you do if you generate extra enquiries but the staff do not deliver as expected? What if you raise the library's profile with the stakeholders who fund you but this new visibility leads them to impose financial cuts?
- Decide how you will measure qualitative and quantitative success in relation to any ambition statement you have drawn up (see Chapter 3). Keep the statement as a guiding principle throughout any outreach activity to help you remember the point of what you are doing. Be alert to mission creep or the drift away from your intended strategy.
- Reflect frequently and evaluate occasionally. Learn always.

Telephone conversations

The telephone is an increasingly resurgent, engaging and powerful communication media in an age when digital communication has become so ubiquitous and varied that any attention is hard won. Telephone conversations allow people to connect with others and are very appropriate where there are complex conversations to be had, particularly in advocacy campaigns. While e-mail and other methods are good for informing stakeholders a two-way dialogue on the telephone helps you to ensure that the information you give them is heard and understood.

Telephone calls are also an important way to build relationships. They add a personal touch to your communication and can create a greater engagement in your stakeholders. The telephone is essential in advocacy where you are trying to persuade rather than just inform. While on a telephone conversation trying to get an appointment you have the chance to respond to objections or other constraints offering further information or persuasion at the time when it is needed. For instance, when contacting a potential partner to discuss a joint approach to a particular initiative, it may become obvious quite quickly that they may not immediately grasp the value for them in the proposal. During a telephone conversation there is the opportunity to react to obvious signs of misunderstanding or add greater persuasive detail where it is needed. With e-mail this can be a long process that can eventually fizzle out or even worse, the e-mail may not have identified the key factors which arose naturally from the telephone conversation. In such cases you may not even get the attention of the potential partner.

If you employ telephone techniques for engagement try not to sound like an employee from a telemarketing company as you may meet significant resistance. If you use an outside agency to make engaging telephone calls then ensure those doing the calls are well trained and genuinely share your enthusiasm and knowledge of library services together with their potentially attractive outcomes.

Interactive non-digital approaches to engagement

There are many non-digital activities that can engage potential users in library contexts:

- Public libraries have a strong and successful history in setting up reading schemes for children, especially over the school summer holidays, and organise book clubs in many countries of the world, from the USA to Hong Kong and New Zealand.
- In the UK, the Reading Agency undertakes an annual Summer Reading Challenge in partnership with public libraries. There is a bright, energetic, interactive, fun website, which is truly engaging, with a programme developing over months each year. In 2020 the programme became digital because of the COVID-19 pandemic. The Reading Agency approach ('tackling life's big challenges through the proven power of

reading') and website (www.readingagency.org.uk) are recommended to all who look for a source of engaging ideas.

■ Competitions and quizzes always engage. Colouring, guessing and scavenger hunts ('can you find?') are simple and popular ways to draw younger people into the library fold. School libraries can offer competitions at various levels of difficulty: make a bookmark; redesign a cover; review a book; write an alternative ending. Library process can be a good source of competition fodder, e.g. design a new library card, make a poster for a library.

■ Although many quizzes and competitions in libraries tend to be for younger age groups they are just as appropriate to engaging adults, for instance they might be attracted by a local history photography competition or similar. Interactivity is the key here and this is made more powerful if aligned with broader cultural events such as World Book Day. Events key to your locality or library sector are likely to be especially appealing for adults.

Digital approaches to engagement are discussed in Chapter 10.

Traditional media

While it is relatively easy to be engaging with face-to-face and other interactive approaches the traditional media are not always suitable for marketing engaging messages, for example because there can be little opportunity for customisation. The challenge is to make traditional media as engaging as possible.

Radio, TV, local and national press, professional journals

Although it is useful to keep journalists fully briefed with press releases and invitations to visit the library, nothing beats securing an invitation for one of your more engaging staff to be on a local radio programme or featured in a printed newspaper or magazine. Local radio is potentially an excellent channel on which to promote libraries as although there is often no visual presentation (sometimes webcams are in radio station studios though), radio draws people close and often has longer guest slots than TV. Guest slots are best used to show the skills and importance of librarians and libraries rather than simply to advertise an event. The librarian as fact searcher, fact checker or reviewer of books is more engaging than the librarian as advertiser.

Print advertisements

The fight for attention in print advertisements is brutal. How many of the advertisements in the last magazine you read can you remember despite the impressive design, colours and energetic language? How many can you remember about topics you only have a vague interest in? Print advertisements are likely only to have significant engagement potential if they are placed where people already have some interest in the topics outlined. They are generally more effective in deepening engagement with existing user groups than with new ones. Unless you have something revolutionary and exciting to say, be prepared to be disappointed by the return from your print advertising campaigns, particularly if they are standalone rather than nested within an integrated marketing campaign.

Leaflet drops

In an increasingly busy and noisy marketing environment it is difficult to make leaflets engaging. There are two main types – those advertising an immediate event and those to be kept for reference. The former only engage if the event is of significant interest to those who have been leafleted; the latter are unlikely to be kept for a future need unless they are for some type of delicious ethnic food. Leaflet drops are best undertaken in the context of a broader campaign that uses more engaging channels, perhaps as a reminder rather than a source of inspiration.

Posters

Like leaflets, posters are usually supportive in the modern marketing environment rather than a main channel of promotional activity. Design and colour can make them striking but they are only engaging if they clearly set out the library's value for those who are looking at them.

Brochures

Provided they are designed and printed to a high standard, brochures can be a useful way to engage users and promote the library. They are unlikely to result in library use in the short term but are useful in building brand and support. They can be handed out to people after outreach or advocacy meetings as a way to reinforce what was said or to impart information. They are likely to have less effect if left around to be picked up by people at random.

Annual reports

For effective advocacy it is essential to produce a well-designed and influential annual report, preferably in printed and digital form. Hand them out after meetings with stakeholders or leave them on stakeholders' desks. Annual reports provide a chance to demonstrate your library's impact and how it is a resource of value. The report should capture attention, stir emotion, and be delivered the way stakeholders prefer to receive it, either in print or digitally. If you have a number of distinct stakeholders with different engagement triggers consider creating separate annual reports, each of which communicates information that is especially relevant to the stakeholder group, while essentially presenting similar facts.

Magazine articles and other editorial material

Magazine editors are acutely aware of the need to be attractive to their readers, so take up any offer to publish in a magazine and use it well. Do not write an article and try to hawk it around a range of magazines, but identify magazines that fit with your chosen user, potential user or stakeholder groups and write for it in the language you think is suitable for them.

Newsletters

Committing to producing a regular newsletter is time-consuming and a potential source of unwanted stress. It is often difficult to sustain momentum and find constantly creative and engaging content. If there is no interesting news then the value of a newsletter may be minimal for the effort it takes to produce. To be attractive the newsletter needs personality, for example success stories about the clear value of the library service to its readers. It can be appealing for named individuals to write regular columns or to include a 'staff picks' type of section. Securing ongoing commitment from library managers to the production of any newsletter is vital. Some library authorities may not approve of individual staff writing in newsletters openly, and this can be a major constraint to engagement.

In-library messaging

The best external communication is wasted if internal library messaging (explicit or implicit) is inconsistent with it. External messages can seek to engage but will fail to do so if a user's experience within the library in question is disappointing.

Displays

Quite often an in-library display, perhaps a book display supported by a pop-up banner, is an excellent opportunity to display engaging library personality. Orkney Public Libraries in Scotland has a reputation for exhibiting humorous displays that are consistent with the joys of reading. Their displays are also re-usable when photographed across a range of social media. Here is some advice to make displays engaging:

- Find out what is interesting to library users or other stakeholders and use knowledge as the basis for most of your displays. For instance, if you are devising a display to accompany an advocacy meeting you could collect evidence to show how the library's aims and objectives fit with those of the stakeholders you are trying to impress. In most cases a display of stock is unlikely to be engaging.
- Although the interests of users or other stakeholders are your key drivers for displays, users are often curious about the staff and their interests, so 'staff picks' can be very engaging. Maybe even devise a system to identify 'user picks' so users can be drawn closer to the library.
- Make it clear what action you want those seeing the display to take. If you make a display of books for loan, advertise clearly that they can be borrowed.
- Use themes that reflect the local life of your users. Health service librarians may provide displays about pandemic responses. A corporate librarian might display items relevant to a recently announced strategic direction for the company. Public librarians might commemorate local events or publicise local authors. The more personal a display is to your users, the more engaging.
- React to recent news, particularly local news, and be ready to create an opportunistic display at all times, even if you have an annual calendar of displays already planned.
- Popular culture can engage the interest of users in public libraries. Themes around TV programmes, films and music stars can often attract. Stay fresh, fun and relevant.
- Consider having bookmarks, reading lists and other takeaways with a printed call to action from your current campaign.
- If it makes sense to include all types of media in a display, do it. But do not confuse users unnecessarily with a variety of materials. Do not allow 'props' to overshadow the display and only use them where they add discreetly to the required overall effect.
- Consider rotating the positioning of displays. Do not use the same space each time as this may result in readers passing by without noticing

changes in content. Make use of areas such as the main entrance, wherever in the library items that are the subject of the display are shelved, or a far corner of the library to draw users deeper into the building.

■ Underpin displays with good graphics, good lighting, good use of colour and simple, warm language. Production values need not be inordinately high but the overall impression should be crisp and neat.

■ Do not allow a display to stay up longer than a few weeks. Familiarity breeds contempt. Keep users' sense of discovery high.

Signage

Signs should send a clear message of welcome and offer guidance on navigating the library and its services in a clear, engaging and unambiguous manner. This is important in academic and public libraries where the physical building may well be multi-floored and daunting. The age of negative signs such as 'Quiet please' or 'Eating food is not allowed in the library' has passed but user experience and engagement is still affected by the quality of wayfinding signage. Here is some advice on making signs engaging:

■ Only use as many signs as are necessary for wayfinding. Do not create more signs than are necessary. If there are too many then users will disengage and feel adrift.

■ Check that the signs throughout the library are consistent in content and style and do not add new ones without checking they fit in.

■ Check all signs are in plain, uncomplicated language. If they are complicated consider whether the journey the user will take through the library is too complicated and needs change.

■ Keep the signs sharp and crisp with a modern look. Passing them every day you may not have noted they have faded or begun to look anachronistic but a new library user will immediately form an impression from such things.

■ Whenever embarking on a signage project do not forget to test the signs before going live. Test with existing users and, if possible, with potential users too. They can give invaluable insights into whether the signage is engaging or disengaging.

Buttons and badges

Although such things may appear to be frivolous never forget that they are fun so deserve your attention to give support in any engagement campaign.

They can be an excellent medium for conveying short snappy messages outlining the benefits of library service. Past examples include 'Librarians – the ultimate search engine', 'Libraries gave us power', 'Support your local library' and 'Reading is for awesome people'. In addition staff lanyards or badges can identify help for users. It is also possible to give digital badges as recognition of participation in an event or programme in a public library or as reward for completing a topic of research in an academic library.

Library guides

Library guides explain how library resources are organised and how users can access them, so they should be designed to be readable and engaging as they are relatively high profile documents. If possible new guides should be tested with various user groups before being made available to make sure they communicate what was intended; if they do not an opportunity to develop a helpful relationship with users will be missed.

The engaging part of the library guide will mainly be the content and how appropriate and interesting it is to those reading it. The potentially disengaging part will mainly be the way that it has been written and presented. Engaging content should not be undermined by poor writing and presentation.

To ensure the document supports the content write clearly and simply, avoid long paragraphs, use a personal tone in writing, with an active rather than passive voice. Use pronouns ('you' is the reader, 'we' is the library), avoid jargon and use the vocabulary of those likely to read the guide.

Profiles of library staff

As engagement with library services often requires a human connection it is worth considering creating publicly available broad profiles of library staff, including photos. Clearly there are privacy issues here and a high staff turnover may make this a non-starter and in some library contexts such personalisation of staff may be more appropriate than in others. Academic libraries, for instance, have liaison librarians and subject specialists who require publicity to encourage people to contact them. It is worth considering publicising a group staff photograph taken in a relatively informal setting to assure readers that they are interacting with a professional and happy team.

A high staff turnover is likely to be a potential barrier to user engagement. It is possible to be engaging without human relationships. Amazon has been especially successful at this, mimicking human interactions with technology in messages encouraging people to buy more from them, such as 'customers who bought this also bought this'. Libraries need personality if they are to be engaging. Personality is usually a human trait not some abstract idea arising from inanimate objects.

Library tours

Think of a library tour as not just an opportunity to provide information on the service and what is where but also as an opportunity to inspire library use by showing personality. Ensure the tour guide is not only knowledgeable about the library but has a genuine love of the services it provides. The vibes and atmosphere that the tour guide creates will stay with those on tour for some time and certainly during their first visits to the library. Try to make sure that responses to questions during the tour create a positive impression.

Self-guided tours can be offered on paper and a variety of technology, including video, which has the valuable characteristic of being able to be stored and re-used in different contexts. However, remember that sometimes the most efficient is not the most engaging. A list of answers to frequently asked questions is not always a satisfactory alternative to being given a personal tour with the opportunity to ask questions of the tour guide.

Messages on promotional items

Promotional items such as pens, mugs, T-shirts, key rings, tote bags and bookmarks are gentle reminders of the brand values inherent in the organisation. While usually not particularly engaging in themselves they may be worth including in a supporting role in a broad campaign. These are better thought of as awareness raising and reminding tools rather than a means of engaging potential library users.

Kiosks

Self-service (issues and returns) and information kiosks are now to be seen in many libraries and potentially increase or reduce the opportunity for engagement. Finding ways to balance their apparent impersonal efficiency with the richer experience possible from offering personal service is likely to be one of the challenges in coming years. Undoubtedly, the need for efficiency, the popularity of technology-based solutions and the COVID-19 pandemic will combine to make kiosks a particularly attractive option for libraries.

There are opportunities to develop some degree of personality within kiosks as newer technologies are introduced. The kiosk may identify you through facial recognition, retina and fingerprint scanning, allowing it to recommend what you might consider reading or consulting next, given your past history of interactions with the library. It is essential to address privacy and similar issues if considering developing the kiosks in this way.

Interactivity is key. Some systems allow users to book meeting rooms and study space (in university libraries), report road maintenance issues, pay council tax or upload details of local events (in public libraries) or disseminate health information (in health service libraries).

Kiosks can be used creatively to develop engagement with specific groups. In 2019 public libraries in Iowa City, Iowa, USA, trialled literary kiosks that promoted literature and local authors. A message on the kiosk asked whether you have one, three or five minutes spare and then printed out a story from a local author of the appropriate length. Kiosks need not be fixed to a specific location but can be mobile, which extends their usefulness.

As the increasing use of self-service and information kiosks in libraries has shown, the future of information and library provision is increasingly likely to be supported by digital channels, which are discussed in the next chapter. The most engaging messaging strategies are likely to be those that employ creative ways to integrate digital and non-digital messaging channels.

10

Digital channels and engagement

At this point in the process of marketing for engagement you now have an overall strategic plan for your engagement and a level of ambition to achieve. Ongoing reflection has allowed this to be informed by a deep understanding of users, potential users and other stakeholders, a clear understanding of the value they seek and how libraries can deliver it to them. A practical segmentation and stakeholder management platform has been considered and a set of engaging messages to each of the segments and stakeholder groups has been devised. A range of channels to convey messages has been identified. What should the contribution of digital marketing, and especially social media, be to your channel strategy?

Creativity can be spurred by unusual events. In 2020, librarians in all sectors across the world rose to meet the issues arising from the COVID-19 pandemic by offering a range of expanded digital services while physical buildings were inevitably closed. Home schooling resources, story times, online conversation groups, online craft sessions and book chats were common public library responses online. Some libraries used Facebook Live and YouTube to present craft videos, using materials that are very common in most homes. Others offered a behind-the-scenes video of the library operations. All types of library found ways to keep contact with their users.

Digital channels offer an opportunity to stay close to users and potential users and to respond swiftly and economically to changing needs and emerging new opportunities. Library websites, social media, video, e-mails, SMS, blogs, podcasts, RSS feeds and chatbots all offer opportunities for libraries to engage with diverse user and potential user groups.

When choosing digital channels library and information professionals should be clear exactly how each one contributes towards an overall engagement strategy. Having an authentic presence on a digital channel needs commitment and it is unlikely that you can offer high levels of commitment across all available channels. In addition, consider that while social media offers the potential for deep engagement with specific groups it is divisive for other groups. Responses to social media are not always neutral and where they are neutral they may not deliver the potential benefits of using the media. Ensure that your chosen audiences are likely to have a positive reaction to library social media activities. Finally, remember that not all potential library users find social media engaging.

To encourage user engagement it is important that library and information staff should themselves be engaged with the library offer. Social media managers need energy and vision, with a little excitement if possible, as managing digital channels is not simply an administrative task. They need to inspire and remain alert to opportunities for last minute unplanned activity that is appropriate and has a positive impact. Managing digital technology requires an unusual balance of innovation and continuity. It is preferable to have a strong presence on a small number of authentic and popular social media platforms rather than be mediocre on a wide range of platforms.

To make the best use of digital channels you need to be clear at the outset what the answers are to these questions:

■ Who uses these channels?
■ Which channels are used by priority segments for engagement?
■ How does this engagement become the beginning of an ongoing conversation rather than simply a channel to inform?
■ How can those receiving the messages via digital channels contribute, interact or co-create through these channels?
■ Will this channel need support from other channels or be standalone?
■ How can engaged users pass on the message promoted by the channel?
■ How will I measure success or otherwise over time?

This chapter gives an overview of the key ways in which digital channels can support engagement activities, and examples of how each support activity can enhance library and information service engagement activities.

The pivotal role of the library website

The library website is likely to be the hub of your digital engagement activity. All social media and apps are likely to offer links to the main website even where they have standalone features too.

For this reason it is important that the website has high-quality relevant content and functions well across browsers and hardware, and has fully working links within a logical and intuitive structure and hierarchy. It needs to be visually attractive and offer an overall great user experience that visitors wish to repeat. Usability studies for engagement need to cover all entry points:

- in the library, where there is help on hand
- remote via computer or tablet
- remote via mobile app.

The website should observe, record and reflect on the experience of different types of searcher with observers and without observers:

- existing users (who have good knowledge of the library and its processes already)
- potential users (who might use the library for a first time)
- library staff (who are the guides through any complexity or misunderstandings).

It is unlikely that a library website can be truly engaging unless it offers some degree of interactivity or co-creation. An interactive website allows users to go beyond simply reading text and viewing images. Instead, interactive websites allow visitors to alter the way in which the website displays, and lets them play games or co-create in various ways.

Important characteristics such as the need to be visually attractive, intuitively structured and technically efficient with all links working are likely to be hygiene factors rather than effective sources of inspiration or engagement in themselves.

Social media is likely to be your main channel for interactivity (e.g. setting up Instagram photo competitions) but there is the opportunity to give your social media posts prominence on the library website, adding energy to what could be simply a professional display of information. In the USA, Clinton Macomb Public Library (www.cmpl.org) has a prominent tab stating 'Get Involved', which links to a number of ways users can become involved with the library service, seek information or borrow items. Involvement and engagement naturally support each other.

The challenge is to make your website into a two-way conversation rather than simply a one-way information dump. Consider how you can build a 'call to action' into your site, which otherwise would be something to read at a distance, for example vote for the next book to read at a children's story time from a series of options, or enter a quiz to test your knowledge of the university's library services.

Judging the success or otherwise of your website ultimately depends on how you have defined engagement for your programme. There are six metrics to consider to help you judge your website's contribution to engagement: the number of returning users, the number of shares, the number of comments, the scroll depth, the average time on page and bounce rate.

Library blogging

Blogs can be posted on websites or independent of them. Library blogs are particularly engaging when produced by librarians who have a strong viewpoint, personality or specialised knowledge as thought leaders. The content of successful blogs would not always be acceptable to a risk-averse library authority, and there can be a challenge in creating an official library blog that is within the library authority or governance culture and also engaging for an audience.

At best, library authority blogs are likely to be mildly engaging channels to convey information while at worst they are time-consuming, uninspired and uninspiring flows of information, which end up moribund after an ever-decreasing frequency of update or valuable content. The more engaging blogs offer content in a variety of forms, including video, podcasts, infographics, stories and interviews with relevant people.

If you decide that your library can sustain a blog then ensure at the outset that the whole library is committed to maintaining it. Provide regular quality content from a broad range of contributors rather than give one enthusiast responsibility for producing it.

While it is necessary to be cautious when deciding whether to start a library blog, it is possible to create and maintain one of high quality. As an example, Queen's University Belfast, Health Care Library (UK), has an excellent blog for healthcare workers (https://blogs.qub.ac.uk/healthcarelibrary/topic/headlines/), and Richmond on Thames Public Library (UK) proves it is possible to sustain high level content through local history and other posts (https://libraryblog. lbrut.org.uk/). The British Library (UK) has a series of blogs ranging from subject areas such as maps (https://blogs.bl.uk/magnificentmaps/) to an intriguing behind-the-scenes look at the workings of the library (https://blogs. bl.uk/living-knowledge/).

Engaging blogs are likely to exhibit a combination of a number of characteristics: have interesting names, include real life stories, be written clearly for a specific audience, offer high-quality content, be regularly updated, actively seek comments.

The major social media

Each of the major social media deserve investigation as contenders for your social media mix. All require significant levels of sustained creativity if used in an attempt to make the library truly engaging. The marketplace for social media attention and interactions is very competitive and just because a library has a social media presence it does not automatically receive the promised or expected benefits from using the social media in question.

Facebook

With over 1.7 billion monthly active users in the third quarter of 2020, Facebook is the biggest social network worldwide (Statista, 2021). To some Facebook is now a little old fashioned and many young people use more visual social media such as YouTube and Instagram. However, despite some organisations reducing their Facebook presence, the platform still has good reach across age groups and merits engagement effort. Facebook groups and Facebook Live have grown significantly recently. Facebook remains a good overall platform for library social media presence allowing a variety of library messaging to be carried via a highly popular platform. Types of library content include: 'how to' help, story times, book reviews, new books forthcoming, trivia questions to highlight library databases on offer, time lapses, animations, memes, 'tell us about' type posts and information about access to the library during various stages of pandemic restrictions and lockdowns.

Flickr and Pinterest

Flickr is a popular space to curate engaging images of the library and its activities. Ensure that you link to Flickr from as many points as possible as it is not often front of mind for potential users. It is possible that people looking for images of libraries to use may make contact and by granting permissions for re-use the library will generate useful publicity.

Pinterest is a useful photo-sharing site where library staff could create virtual bookshelves, or post pictures of successful events and other activities for followers or general searchers. The photos can be organised into 'boards'. Never underestimate the value of picture and photo-sharing websites.

Instagram and Snapchat

Instagram and Snapchat are photo- and video-sharing platforms, which allow users to send messages, photos or video. Instagram is ideally suited to demonstrate the professionalism of staff, for example by promoting special books and events, giving users and potential users a behind-the-scenes look at library operations, or showing sessions held at library conferences. A 'sneak peek' is often engaging. Instagram Stories allows users to create transient 'day in the life' type reels and slideshows that vanish after 24 hours. Instagram Live can be used at library events to inform followers what is going on. Although it is a little more time-consuming to load content onto Instagram than Snapchat, the former has various advantages for libraries: it is curated, uses hashtags and geotags, links can be included in the profile and everyone can see likes and comments.

Snapchat has a younger user base than Instagram, is not curated and is relatively ephemeral. Nevertheless, it may be used to contact some hard to reach segments, as long as library staff ensure they are authentic on the platform.

LinkedIn

This is useful if your engagement programme involves targeting the business community. Posts need to be business-like and engaging, not simply generally informational. Explain clearly how it would help business people to engage with the library in order to achieve their goals, for example through giving them new ideas about how to run a profitable business or how to develop their careers.

Reddit

The news aggregator and discussion forum Reddit is conveniently structured in a network of communities. Registered members submit content such as posts, links and images or memes to the site, which are then voted up or down by other members. There are 'subreddits' (posts organised by subject) for libraries and librarians and excellent opportunities for social listening in broader library engagement planning. While Reddit is not as popular as Facebook and Twitter, it offers good access to a specific group of users and potential users.

TikTok

TikTok is a truly engaging short-form video-sharing platform. Information sharing about libraries needs to be very creative to be successful on this dynamic platform. Short, fun and energetic snippets from library events and activities might be appropriate as a small part of an engagement action plan for TikTok. Some of the more interesting uploads to the platform have been of individuals or groups choosing from a catalogue of music and comedy dialogues to present hilarious parodies.

Although this degree of fun is not necessary in a shared video, TikTok is certainly not an obvious medium on which to simply upload a short library-promotional video. Arguably, this medium requires more creativity than any other of the social media if it is to be effective as part of a marketing and engagement strategy. While librarians are still trying to understand their authentic place within TikTok, a simple search for 'library' on TikTok shows that libraries can generate huge numbers of likes, way in excess of what can be expected from some traditional social media.

Twitter

Well established for short-form blog texts, Twitter has become an essential channel of communication for many libraries as it is an ideal channel on which to engage in pithy memes (see the section 'Promote library personality' later in the chapter for more on these). Make sure that followers engage with your posts. Even if you have a good number of followers there is the potential for 'tweeting into the void', so likes, and particularly comments, are the most useful metrics. Be sure to get the best out of Twitter by using hashtags, completing the description and location in your account details, and most importantly contributing to any conversation that arises from comments on your posts.

YouTube

Video content is usually, though not always, much more engaging than textual content. YouTube is the most popular video platform and the second most visited website after Google. There is an opportunity to build an engaged YouTube community but this is highly dependent on being able to provide consistently relevant, regularly updated, content. The ability to archive materials shown on your channel allows them to be viewed multiple times. YouTube has recently been challenged in the market by short-form video platforms such as Instagram and TikTok and broader streaming services such as Facebook Live.

Zoom

The online meeting platform Zoom became very popular during the COVID-19 pandemic of 2020 as libraries reflected on how to run events when physical access to libraries was discouraged or prohibited. Mount Prospect Public Library (https://mppl.evanced.info/signup/) in Illinois, USA, has used Zoom to run a programme of events and activities. It allows book pick-ups from the library to be scheduled, and enables book clubs, computer software lessons, crafts sessions, baby and toddler story times, a Pokémon club and meetings with council officials to take place online.

Other platforms

In addition to these standard social media platforms, librarians should stay alert to other emerging platforms:

- Nextdoor is valuable to find local information and learn about what is important in the community at the moment. It is currently available in Australia, Canada, Denmark, France, Germany, Italy, the Netherlands, Spain, Sweden, the UK and the US.
- Quora has over 300 million active users and is a platform where they ask and answer questions. Librarians may consider joining an occasional conversation as part of a social listening strategy.
- Tribe offers secure online spaces to collect insights from users, or can be left more open as a library community space.
- Discord, 'Your Place to Talk and Hang Out', is essentially for gamers but has the potential to be used for book clubs and other groups created by libraries.
- Kahoot! is a game-based classroom platform for administering quizzes, facilitating discussions or collecting survey data. Some public, academic and school libraries are experimenting with posting quizzes on this platform.

This list will be quickly out of date as new platforms emerge and others become absorbed into broader platforms. Wherever people meet online there is always an opportunity to see how library staff can use the platform to their advantage, so consider each new platform as it emerges for its library engagement potential. In all this swirling change do not forget that simple is often best and long established tools such as Messenger and WhatsApp may well be useful. The sheer complexity of digital channels available requires good scheduling. Integration and scheduling software such as that provided by Hootsuite or Buffer is available to help take the drudgery out of this task.

How social media platforms support libraries' engagement activities

Once you are confident that your website and any supporting blogs are well aligned with your engagement ambitions, it is time to choose an appropriate and authentic social media presence. This section outlines the contribution that social media can make to engagement, the major social media platforms for library activity, and gives examples of how the platforms can help libraries achieve the stated benefits.

These are ten ways in which social media can be used to support engagement activities:

- *Increase awareness of the library and its services.* This is fundamental as before users or supporters can engage in any meaningful way their interest must be sparked so they recognise a desire to know more about what is on offer. None of this is possible if they are unaware of the library and the value it can bring to their lives.
- *Keep in regular contact with stakeholders.* Many people access their social media at least once per day, often many more times. This provides the opportunity for library staff to post a number of gentle 'touches' over time, which if received positively support engagement objectives. They need not post a set number of times per day but when there is occasion to do so, and make sure information given is updated when necessary. There is nothing sadder and more uninspiring than a website, Twitter account or Facebook page that hasn't been updated for weeks.
- *Promote library services and give basic information about its range of products.* Traditional marketing channels can also do this but social media are especially appropriate to convey feelings and emotions. On social media you need a brand voice with appropriate character and personality (friendly, inspiring, authoritative, warm), tone (humble, direct, honest), language (simple, fun) and purpose (engaging, entertaining).
- *Be recognised as a thought leader in some area of interest to those accessing social media.* There are many areas where library and information professionals could position themselves as thought leaders, especially in these political and economic times when facts often seem to be blurred by emotion.
- *Encourage word-of-mouth recommendations.* 'Liking' or forwarding a social media post is an ideal way to promote the library. A friend's social share acts as a pre-screening recommendation and can encourage deeper engagement.
- *Provide access to influencers.* Some social media users influence others and giving them access can help with wider engagement objectives.

However, influencers realise their power so it is vital if you take this approach that you have something appropriate to offer them.

■ *Use social listening to gauge sentiment towards the library.* Social listening is the practice of tracking conversations that revolve around specific words or phrases. You can then use these words and phrases to develop new opportunities specifically for those audiences. Where authentic and within the library's social media policy, you can even use their vocabulary in messages to them. As noted earlier, engagement is encouraged as much by emotion as it is by rational argument. Social media can make a significant contribution to assessing positive or negative emotions towards the library. Collect and preserve all social media comments that praise the library and, most importantly, any that note the positive influence the library service has had on an individual's life. Sometimes there are posts on social media noting when somebody has achieved something of importance to them such as reading a book from the library or using a digital information source.

■ *Provide deep general knowledge of users' and potential users' feelings.* Conversations via social media can sometimes give you a much deeper general knowledge of users' and potential users' feelings than any traditional survey could ever do.

■ *Make your engagement activities more efficient.* Engagement activities can be made more efficient by storing records of events. For example, storing YouTube and Facebook Live events makes them available for multiple viewings at diverse times, allowing users and other stakeholders to engage at times other than the original broadcast date.

■ *Encourage increased activity and support.* Whatever performance measures you have as a library, social media enables you to measure responses to library activity, whether website traffic, or attendance at online or other events.

Having considered the benefits social media can bring to the library and looked at the major features of the main social media, here are specific examples of how libraries have used social media to support engagement activities.

Increase general awareness

At their most basic social media platforms can be used to develop awareness, as a simple advertising medium where general library information and details of events and services can be distributed. These are some real Twitter and Facebook posts that increase general awareness of the library:

Here are just a few of over 20 Lego e-book titles available to borrow from our e-library.

UK public library

Do you work in an administrative role in an academic library? Why not join your peers from across [the region] in an experience sharing event on 15 July? Further information, and how to book your place, can be found here.

UK academic library group

Several regional & branch libraries open to the general public as of Friday, 26th June, 2020 onwards, depending on the respective library's opening hours.

USA public library

Although not exciting or full of personality, such social media messages build awareness of the library. Sometimes important messages are displayed, as in the range of recent videos available online from particular libraries outlining post-pandemic re-opening arrangements and requirements. Many are friendly in tone, posted with a light 'we can't wait to welcome you back' touch to recognise and reinvigorate relationships with library users.

Information and awareness messages underpin a broad annual engagement campaign and alert those who receive the message to specific events or offers. A stream of such informational messages is unlikely to be engaging so the overall campaign managers should present ideas, interactivity and personality through other means.

Keep in regular contact with those you wish to engage with

Many people dip into their various social media accounts several times per day. Anecdotal evidence suggests that it often takes seven touches to elicit some sort of reaction from potential stakeholders so bear this in mind. It is important to use social media within an integrated campaign across a small number of carefully chosen platforms rather than simply on one platform such as Twitter or Facebook.

If you focus on one or two key platforms when promoting a campaign try also to experiment with using an emerging platform, such as TikTok, which appeals to one of your key user groups. The emerging platform is unlikely to be your main channel for communicating but it will add a new dimension and might encourage deeper engagement from a hard to reach user group. For example you might consider a low-key platform such as Discord, Kahoot! or Jackbox to see if you fit with their users. Do not be surprised though if you get no immediate response. Reflect and learn from the experience from the positives or negatives. You will find that this type of social media platform often has a short life until a dominant channel emerges, so be prepared to follow its evolution if you find it satisfactory.

Promote library personality

What sort of library personality is promoted during a library social media campaign? How is the library to be presented and how does it wish to be perceived? How do users and other stakeholders relate to the library and their expectations of it? Given the variety of pictorial, movie and textual opportunities in social media there is the opportunity for well-rounded approaches to conveying personality.

Is the library trying to communicate that it is fun? Erudite? Caring? Alert and up to date? Relevant to users or other stakeholders? The library can be different things to different people but it is very important that the right people receive the right messages through the right media. Confused messages are likely to distance users and other stakeholders rather than engage them, so plan detailed, wide-ranging campaigns.

TikTok is good at communicating personality through short video posts, but it can be challenging to find library messages that communicate well on such a medium. It is not well suited to detailed or informational messaging. A search for library-related content on TikTok shows that there is high potential for engagement for those who manage to align with the culture underpinning the platform.

Here is an overview of some library-related content on TikTok. Likes were counted in early December 2020:

- Book processing in the library. 25,000 likes. Compare that to Facebook or Twitter volumes of likes for any specific post. The TikTok clip simply shows the process of putting plastic covers on new books.
- Reader quietly walks around the shelves at Cornell University Library (USA) showing the beautiful architecture and trying not to disturb those working. 115,000 likes.
- 'Libraries are my favourite places. Libraries I want to visit before I die.' Short compilation of beautiful library architecture. 22,000 likes.

The dynamism of TikTok attracts posts that include descriptions of readers doing unusual things, sometimes in quiet, less visited, parts of the library, for example laminating a cracker in a high school library (311,000 likes) or going to the library desk to ask for ridiculous book titles (114,000 likes).

One technique that libraries have embraced is the creation of memes, which offer the opportunity to express feeling, show personality and, importantly, create something that people pass on to others because it is funny or profound. A meme is usually a visual idea (a photo or video), behaviour or style that offers pointed commentary on social ideas, current events or cultural symbols. In the library context these are often intended to be funny, with an important library-related point behind them, for example:

- a picture of a hand pointing towards the shelves with the text, 'Alternative facts can be found in our fiction section' (academic library, UK)
- two books on the artist Monet with the Twitter text, 'Here she comes now saying' (UK public library)
- a picture of a dinosaur with the text, 'Dinosaurs didn't read. Now they are extinct. Thank goodness the thesaurus survived' (widely used).

Memes should not be thought of as witty adverts but as engaging cultural commentary. Library staff should be careful, though, as the most effective memes can be divisive and based on edgy content. However, there is great opportunity to create interesting memes around the misunderstandings that people have about libraries. Blank meme templates to stimulate your own thinking are available at https://imgflip.com/memetemplates and https://giphy.com.

Be recognised as a thought leader

Social media platforms can lead and manage discussion on relevant topics and provide an opportunity for the library service to display its expertise. This does not have to be a final pronouncement on an age old philosophical problem and can be as simple as posting a regular Instagram, Twitter or Flickr post of old photographs, which the archivist has diligently curated over a long period of time. New York Public Library has an excellent Flickr account on which photographs of old New York are displayed. They prompt detailed discussion and engagement with various aspects of the city's history and the public library. The library is a central facilitator of this conversation with significant forwarding of photos and referencing the library collection of local history images. In addition New York Public Library has over 2.5 million followers who receive details of the library's recommendations for 'book of the day', which position the library as a thought leader in reading opportunities.

However, the real magic of New York Public Library's use of social media is its ability to make everything, from posts about erudite research bibliographies to retweeting a news story on David Bowie's favourite books, seem part of a natural, integrated whole. This professionalism is not guaranteed to deliver high activity in all performance indicators, however. In the month's worth of tweets researched during the writing of this book the number of retweets rarely exceeded 20–50 out of 2.5 million followers. 'Likes' rarely reached 100. One notable exception was when there were 115 retweets for a library call for stories from 'History Now – the Pandemic Diaries Project'. This supports the belief that those reading messages on Twitter are more likely to act (by retweeting) when asked to do something practical than to retweet messages that are purely informational. Though you should not have too high an expectation of the countable results of your social media activity there is genuine value in this degree of engagement in the overall positioning in the mind of users and potential users.

Encourage word-of-mouth recommendations

'Likes', shares and retweets are an obvious way to encourage word-of-mouth recommendation, but may not be attracted easily. The sheer number of followers an account has does not necessarily translate into significant likes or shares. And as Facebook is now driven by algorithms to identify 'meaningful interactions' your message may not get the full distribution you expected from your follower base. Make sure followers have a reason to be inspired to pass on a post you wish to spread. Sometimes this can be achieved by developing linked Facebook groups to communicate with specific groups of users who are likely to share interests and know others with the same interests. Norfolk Library and Information Services (UK), for instance, has added to its generic site the related groups Norfolk Libraries for Families, Norfolk Borrowers (for those who want to share thoughts on books they read but can't attend book groups) and an all age e-book reading group (mainly for children aged 8–11, with support from parents). Separate Facebook pages exist for the major libraries such as the Norwich Millennium Library, one of the busiest public libraries in the UK. This encourages users and potential users to relate to their local library or primary need for the library and thus underpins engagement potential.

Give access to influencers

People tend to be influenced by people they like or respect. Delivering library communications through such people can be a great way to achieve engagement. A very high proportion of people trust recommendations from people they know over more general promotional activity so engaging with influencers and other people 'like me' is an excellent way to encourage library ideas to spread.

This approach is noticeable in UK academic libraries where library champions have been widely adopted. For example, in Bangor University, as part of the university-wide Student Engagement Unit the Student Library Champions 'work to put students' views at the heart of improving the library and archives service'. This type of approach is ideal for social media activities where students can contact, support and inspire other students 'like me'.

Library and Knowledge Services (LKS) at Nottinghamshire Healthcare NHS Foundation Trust (UK) have become Digital Champions for the whole organisation. This positions the library as a major source of expertise in supporting IT skills development organisation-wide. In addition to the British Columbia (Canada) example given earlier (see p. 133), a number of public library services throughout the world are also showing interest in library champions. In early 2021 at least one library authority in the UK was advertising for volunteers to become library champions. Many library associations have engaged the support of local and national celebrities to champion the values of libraries to their communities.

Every librarian is aware of library users who have benefited from the library and have a story to tell. With the co-operation of the storytellers, who are often more than willing to share their story in support of the library, these stories make engaging social media posts. In January 2021 the phrase 'the library helped me' returned over 18,000 hits on google.co.uk, including the following, each of which could be the beginning of an engaging story for social media:

> The library helped me believe in myself.
> How the library helped me connect with my Chinese father.
> The library helped me to integrate.
> The library helped me to learn so many new skills that are still listed on my resumé to this day.
> The library helped me start my business.
> Three hours at the library helped me cool off the sounds of the day and brought me to a more peaceful, balanced state of mind before bedtime.

In this world of celebrity endorsement, involving celebrities in any social media campaign is a great opportunity. If you see celebrities making comments about libraries, particularly local celebrities making comments about your library, do not be afraid to ask them for their endorsement as part of your engagement campaign. Libraries are institutions that have a history of inspiring people to great achievements. If this local endorsement is not possible then stay alert on Twitter and look for library champions whose posts you can retweet. Not only will you be emphasising the good in libraries but you will also be creating some degree of engagement with those who are your potential allies.

Encourage social listening and gauge sentiment

Monitor each of your social media choices as well as those you do not have a presence with to find out what users are saying about libraries and their values. Social listeners monitor what is being said and look for root causes behind the content of social conversations, then use them to build better engagement strategies. For instance, a company librarian may note that various user groups in the company's markets are complaining about another company's offerings. This provides opportunities for reflection and realignment of corporate library services to look for opportunities in areas of the market where needs are not met. Thus the librarian can position the service as part of the value creation by the business rather than simply as a cost in maintenance expenditure for collections and staff. The outcome could well be greater engagement with users and the key stakeholders responsible for funding.

Social listening tools include Social Mention, HubSpot, Sprout Social, Keyhole and Awario. They commonly offer keyword searching and some let users analyse textual and other content of posts, or offer a view on the degree of positivity, negativity or neutrality within the texts on specific subjects.

Some snippets don't make national headlines but are picked up by local social media. In November 2020, Social Mention ('real-time social media search and analysis') indexed a blog that, among other things, revealed an example of an opportunity for engagement: 'Fairfax County Public Library [Virginia, USA] will reduce fines up to $15 for food donations during December'. Listening to what other libraries have done, and the reactions to their activities, can spark new ideas for your own engagement activities.

Social Mention indexed 71 occurrences of 'library' in November 2020: 21 positive, 45 neutral, 5 negative. The term 'library' can be used in many contexts so take care when interpreting this sentiment data.

Social media can be brutal and the source of unsubstantiated criticism. Misunderstandings and misinformation can be gently corrected by speedy response online. In addition to general and analytical monitoring by social media tools as noted above, digital channels give library staff an opportunity to clarify misunderstanding on social media, as evidenced by comments on Facebook, Twitter and other platforms. Library staff are ill advised to get involved in any argument through social media, but should use their platform to point out errors and misunderstandings calmly. Without social media there are few opportunities to respond to misunderstandings quickly, many of which may never surface through traditional channels.

Give deeper general knowledge of the feelings of users and potential users

Quick real-time surveys and ongoing collection of unsolicited website comments can deepen your knowledge of customer needs, wants, attitudes and perceptions. Online surveys are traditionally used to test satisfaction with an existing part of service or to ask library users about potential choices ahead. For instance, the choice of future marketplace resource guides produced by a corporate library could be decided well in advance by a voting procedure online, which offered two or three alternatives. The most popular choice determines what sort of resource guide is compiled. This exercise also provides useful general information for library staff about what is likely to be popular in the future, perhaps in a more sophisticated way than simply asking users what they want through a traditional survey. It offers the opportunity to discuss a matter with users and potential users who are geographically distributed and may be solitary.

As with many aspects of engagement strategy, the use of surveys via social media encourages new and creative uses of a traditional approach to understanding users' needs and wants. Users can be invited to participate in fun activities such as a quiz and to encourage their friends to join in too. This potentially widens the library audience into areas previously not considered.

Surveys can help to provide an information base as an input into a quick response to key issues that arise. Library authorities and professional library associations throughout the world used tools such as SurveyMonkey to canvass opinion quickly on what the priorities were of readers and staff during the COVID-19 pandemic of 2020. In a pre-social-media era this would not have been so easy or quick to undertake.

Software to help you create online surveys includes Google Forms, SmartSurvey, SurveyLegend, SurveyMonkey, SurveyPlanet and Typeform. Many of these combine free and paid services dependent on the degree of sophistication and number of respondents you expect.

Make your engagement activities more efficient

There is often pressure on library resources and many have found it difficult to support marketing and engagement activities to the extent that they need to, to be truly effective. Social media helps libraries to act faster and deeper than traditional media, offering good value for money. Here are examples of how it does this:

- You can archive your most engaging library activities for multiple uses 24/7.
- Chatbots enable you to respond quickly to queries and communicate in real time.
- Encouraging users to share your content makes it go further at no extra cost.
- Real-time information enables you to be data driven in your message planning at minimum cost.

Integrating all this can seem a really difficult and time-consuming task. Not surprisingly library suppliers offer a range of automated tools and techniques to deliver the potential efficiencies of social media. The Online Computer Library Center's (OCLC's) Wise, for instance, can support a public library's social media strategy by managing all the transactional data produced through library service to create an understanding of users, which will be very useful in finalising social media strategy.

Encourage increased activity and support

Ultimately one of the best outcomes from social media is increased use of libraries and support for libraries. In addition to generally advertising events and new resources in expectation of greater take-up of the offer, there is opportunity for great creativity in encouraging increased use. For example, social media can be used to offer quizzes, which require the use of library resources.

Deciding which social media platforms to communicate through is very important when creating an engagement strategy. Use Table 10.1 to help you

Table 10.1 *Topics to think about when choosing social media platforms*

	Facebook	YouTube and TikTok	Twitter, Instagram and Snapchat	Pinterest and Flickr
Audience (who?)				
Purpose (why?)				
Frequency (when?)				
Engaging content (what?)				
Message types (e.g. photo, text, video, survey, quiz, other)				
Opportunities for co-creation (e.g. conversation)				
Management and measurement tools				

choose the best platforms for any particular audience. A platform that is engaging may not necessarily have high production values.

Although Table 10.1 suggests Facebook; YouTube and TikTok; Twitter, Instagram and Snapchat; Pinterest and Flickr, these platforms can be swapped for others you choose.

Social media policies and guidelines

Policies are important to settle disputes externally (e.g. what can be said through the library's social media accounts) and guide what library staff can and should be doing with social media (e.g. what should they post). Given library governing bodies are likely to be relatively risk averse the policy is a guide for staff and to protect the library when interacting with users online.

A policy and guidelines document might include sections on any of the following subjects: purpose and scope, audience, staff responsibilities, the complaints procedure, what is considered acceptable behaviour, a disclaimer and privacy statements, hints for creating engaging and attractive social media posts. These are discussed below.

Purpose and scope

There is a range of possible community engagement levels available to libraries and the policy and guidelines document should set out clearly what users or potential users can expect from its social media presence. How interactive can social media users expect the library to be? The library might:

- post information related to its services and operations for its users and potential users but not seek out or respond to comments
- invite people to post or comment occasionally on various issues and may respond or join in a conversation
- positively engage with its community on matters relating to the library's resources and services.

Audience

It is useful to identify who the social media content is created for. A public library authority may identify their audience as those people residing within their local authority area, while an academic library may define its intended audience as university students, faculty, staff, administrators and alumni. Often, although these may be the core audience, libraries – particularly special- ised libraries – include others who are interested in its mission and values.

Staff responsibilities

Each social media account is a digital face of the library and the quality of digital customer services should be the same as that in any physical library. The policy should outline appropriate staff behaviour and responsibilities in social media activities. Make clear that all staff should apply the policy guidelines consistently.

Complaints procedure

Deal with complaints in a structured and fair way. The social media policy document should outline the procedure and timescales.

Acceptable behaviour and its consequences

Social media is often a shining example of co-operation and co-creation but it sometimes has a less positive side. Defining acceptable behaviour while retaining the engaging side of social media is a constant challenge. As library governing bodies tend to be risk averse, set out in detail in the policies and guidelines document what is considered acceptable behaviour, and what the consequences are of contravening the guidelines. Here is one such detailed page on a UK county council library Facebook page:

> And now for the dull but important disclaimers! [The]Library and Information Service is not responsible for the accuracy of messages posted by contributors on this Facebook site. The Library and Information Service reserves the right to remove users or messages from the site and to determine what type of information is considered appropriate. Unsuitable content includes:
> - Any sensitive personal data
> - Any material in violation of any laws (including copyright)
> - Sexist, racist, pornographic, gambling, advertising, political, indecent or abusive messages or material.
>
> Links to external pages are provided for the convenience of users and no responsibility is assumed by [the] Library and Information Service for content provided by external websites linked to these pages.
>
> Facebook, [2021]

At the other extreme many engaging non-library Facebook group pages go for a simpler 'keep it friendly, happy and free from advertising' approach. It is unlikely any library would be allowed to be so succinct or loose. However, when developing your policy statements remember that the tone of your language influences the degree to which users engage with you.

Disclaimer and privacy statements

Social media is potentially a legal nightmare. Any social media policy should make it clear that posts by users do not reflect the views of library services, officers or staff. Library disclaimers should reflect current privacy best practice and make it clear that it will not collect any personally identifiable information or sell it to third parties. Issues around copyright and the use of illustration, including permissions for photographs of attendees at library events, also have to be fully understood. It is very important that when devising your policy and guidelines you seek advice from the legal department within your institution.

When completed your social media policy should be made available on your website and signposted from appropriate other platforms. It is almost inevitable that, given the nature of social media, you have to manage disputes and potentially serious unacceptable behaviour. Think about this before committing to using social media and have a clear statement of policy for all to see and work from.

Practical hints for writing engaging social media posts

These are some key tips on how to use social media to support engagement:

- Listen before you talk. You have one mouth and two ears. Spend twice as much time on listening to the chatter on social media as you do posting to it.
- Track library relevant conversations across the internet not just in library accounts.
- Do not feel you have to have a presence on all social media platforms. It is better to have a strong presence on one or two platforms than to be mediocre across the board on many.
- Take part in online conversations on your media platforms. If someone retweets one of your posts, thank them and consider retweeting their posts. If someone posts on your Facebook page respond with some conversation. Remember you are not achieving the benefits of social media if you treat it simply as an electronic poster board. Engage if you expect to be engaged with.
- If you are promoting events do not simply use social media to give details. Suggest interactivity – encourage people to post live tweets, or suggest that they take photos and post them to your Facebook page. And complete the cycle by blogging about it yourself after the event.
- Create competitions, quizzes and other interactive posts.

- Although you should always be aware of the production values of the items you film, remember that sometimes an iPhone video is sufficient to convey your message.
- Do not forget the importance of the background in any video you shoot. If you are reading a story about farmyard animals it is appropriate to film it out in the countryside with animals in the background. Do not feel that you always need to have the library as background. It is usually what the library does that is engaging rather than the physical library, unless the library is incredibly physically attractive to those the video or photographs are aimed at.
- Remember that although you will find lots of (sometimes conflicting) advice on the internet there is no one guaranteed time of day or day of the week to get the highest response to your social media posts. Experiment. What works for those you wish to engage with? Social media is as much an art as it is a science.
- Seek permission from attendees at events to feature them in your social media posts. Human elements make posts engaging.
- And remember – your post must be truly valuable to the people reading your social media.

A social media engagement campaign should not be instituted unless it is fully resourced. In addition to design and development costs do not underestimate the need to staff the programme appropriately. It should not be the responsibility of one social media enthusiast. Have a number of people working as a team in administration, content creation and development.

As one of the attractions of social media is its immediacy, ensure that you have more than one member of administrative staff, perhaps three, to cover new comments and posts. Hold a regular, perhaps monthly, social media meeting to identify the themes and features to be scheduled for the coming period. Build flexibility into the scheduling so that quick opportunistic reactions can be made to events as they appear and unfold.

Do not underestimate how long it takes for people to respond to your digital efforts. It seems an immediate medium but this is often for the sensational rather than simple, creative library activities.

Here are some tips for how to consider the place of social media in your engagement strategy:

- As far as possible, make sure you have a clear idea of your library's goals for the coming one and three years.
- Assess how your priorities fit with each of the user groups and social media platforms and be clear what you expect each to do (e.g. Twitter

gives regular informational updates, YouTube provides live streaming from events and archives them, Instagram conveys atmosphere and personality through pictures).
■ Make your choice of medium and a plan for content, scheduling and staffing.
■ Do not be fooled into thinking there is the one true way to manage your social media – stay experimental to some degree.
■ Keep your nerve! Do not expect or plan for instant results but hope to create buzz.

Digital support for engagement strategies
The contribution of e-mail

Regardless of library sector e-mail is no longer an exciting medium but may well be worth considering as part of a wider campaign. Use e-mails if you expect recipients to do something almost immediately as it is unlikely that they will keep your e-mail with an offer 'just in case' or feel the need to file messages which are simply to be used 'if ever you need us'. Research into users' needs and upcoming life events so e-mails you send them are highly relevant to what is happening in their lives now.

Expect only 20–30% of your e-mails will be opened, but hope for a higher opening rate. Use e-mail mainly for existing users where you may get a higher opening rate. After all, these people, as existing users are probably already engaged with your library to some extent and with any luck feel communications from you are worth opening because past experience has shown that your communications are interesting and relevant to them.

If you intend to start a broad e-mail marketing campaign beyond existing users (and within data protection law) be aware that to get any degree of engagement your posts need to be persuasive rather than simply informational. To be persuasive you need a clear offer and reason why e-mail recipients need to take up that offer now, not at some point in the future. Given the low opening rates e-mail is not a very good tool for simply developing awareness.

Look at your analytics in whatever social media platforms you are using to reveal user engagement by day, time and demographic. Then frame your strategy based on the day or time you have the highest returns.

Here is a basic checklist of questions that you should challenge yourself with to ensure you get the best out of any library e-mail campaign:

■ What are you are trying to achieve and how does the campaign align to library engagement goals? Will you know when you have achieved it?

- Is your contact list segmented so that you can reach those you intend to and not waste time on those who will not benefit from your offer?
- Is the e-mail list clean? Are the e-mail addresses verified and current without duplicates?
- Is the subject line engaging and clear? Does it convey a sense of urgency through a crisp 'call to action'? Does it convey really important value for those who receive it?
- Would you bother to open it yourself if you were part of the targeted e-mail list?
- Have you tested technical aspects of the mail before sending it, ensuring it has no typos; no bad links; no images that will not load; works across desktop, mobile and tablet, and for various e-mail clients?
- Are sentences short and energetic rather than long and dry?
- Has the time of day and day of the week has been considered for delivery?
- Have clear meaningful metrics been devised and a process for monitoring and realignment been agreed?
- Does it fit within national privacy and copyright legislation and regulations?
- Is it within regulations and guidelines set by your funding body?

E-mail can be useful in libraries to:

- inform users when new books and other resources are added to stock which fit with their profile; this profile has to be set up by users and as far as possible managed by them
- alert users to impending due dates for materials they have out on loan
- alert users when reservations are ready to collect
- remind attendees of an approaching event
- allow users to book space on computers or rooms.

E-mail newsletters can be a useful addition to your engagement strategy but beware that they are time-consuming and require a good throughput of interesting and highly relevant content. If you do not have a strong stream of interesting, evolving content then seriously question why anyone would want to read your newsletter. One area where a newsletter might prove particularly useful is in supporting company project teams in corporate library settings. This gives the librarian an opportunity to stay front of mind with team members even when they do not make contact for help in accessing specific information.

Software to help you design and deliver e-mail newsletters is constantly evolving. Some names to investigate now are: Smore, Flipsnack, Canva, Animoto, SendGrid, LibraryAware, Emma, Mailchimp, Constant Contact,

Patron Point, Savannah by OrangeBoy. Blog support is possible via WordPress, Blogger and Wix. Each one has its own features and benefits depending on the type of e-mail newsletter programme you wish to use.

The contribution of mobile apps to engagement strategies

If library staff want to engage with their users and stakeholders they should consider creating a highly specific mobile app. Such technology offers the potential for fast, efficient and increasingly personalised access to library services. It is undeniable that many people now live their lives through mobile phone screens, and many websites are optimised for mobile in such a way that the mobile version is superior to the desktop and laptop or even tablet versions.

People are very engaged with their mobile phones and it would be foolish for libraries not to embrace this technology as a key part of the communication chain with users. It is likely that over the next few years there will be significant app development and innovation within the library market in an attempt to engage through convenience and speed of action and add new dimensions to library service. In addition to making an efficient front end to the administrative aspects of library service there is also the opportunity through push notifications to keep in regular contact with users, however remote. Opportunities also exist for instant user polling as an input to dynamic library planning.

General public library apps already in existence include BorrowBox, Spydus Mobile and MyLibrary! BorrowBox offers curated digital e-books and e-audiobook content for loan activated by public library membership details:

> Our vision has always been to create a digital experience for libraries and library members that rivals consumer brands. To create a user experience that is world class – designed to be simple and made to inspire
>
> BorrowBox, 2020

If your library uses Spydus software you can access Spydus Mobile, which allows you to search your library for books, e-books, DVDs, music and other resources, then download, save or reserve the items. A 'discover' feature offers personalised recommendations. Similar to Spydus Mobile, MyLibrary! offers comparable app functionality for Polaris and Sierra library partners. Such apps integrate the library environment with the wider environment. For instance barcodes can be scanned in bookshops or elsewhere and the app can reveal whether the book is in library stock, allowing immediate reservation. All this functionality is underpinned with administrative details of your library account, which you can update.

In addition to these mainly public library apps many academic libraries have their own library apps, which in addition to the general functionality described above also give access to reading lists for individual modules, course timetables and room bookings for group or individual study. Health libraries and co-operative groups within health libraries have also created apps with access to e-books and e-journals. A remarkable health libraries app is provided by the Princess Royal University Hospital Library in the UK. This app offers a substantial curated collection of medical and health information.

Anyone considering digital channels for their library services and collections increasingly puts app development at the centre of their thinking. Apps offer the potential for a truly customised, convenient and engaging experience, despite the possibility of teething problems in their early development. Users of digital services can be very critical, and unforgiving of imperfections and awkwardness in the way the app operates, even when the digital version clearly adds new convenience to the delivery of library services. An increasingly important skill for librarians in the age of the app is to manage the tension between user expectations and user experience effectively.

Digital approaches to library service offer outstanding opportunities for creativity and engagement potential. Although these are constrained by the concerns and values of funding bodies, there will be a push towards engaging with the very human side of social media. Already we are seeing Spotify playlists created by librarians and Instagram Stories being developed. Digital and social media increasingly offer the opportunity for users and potential users to allow librarians to engage more deeply into their everyday lives.

Having chosen the channels and messages, the engagement programme can now be run through an action plan within a marketing plan framework. The final two chapters of this book offer advice on evaluating the programme (Chapter 11) and ensuring your programme has the best chance of success (Chapter 12).

11

Evaluating the response to engagement activity

Measuring and evaluating user and other stakeholder engagement with the library and its services is fraught with difficulties. Which indicators are appropriate and worthwhile? What levels of performance against these would be considered good? If measuring external engagement should you also measure employee engagement with the library purpose, its services and users? Having engaged users but disengaged staff is unlikely to provide the environment where the library service fulfils its engagement ambitions.

Despite these difficult questions, it is important to find a meaningful way to measure our progress in increasing levels of engagement. This is important for two reasons:

- In most library contexts there is a need to show through measurement that resources and funding have been spent and used wisely.
- We need to learn from our past activities. If marketing activities are not closely evaluated how will we know what works and what does not, with the consequent implications and advice for future activity?

Even though a library's goals may not be fully reached, progress towards achieving them may well be sufficient to constitute success when routes to engagement are long and unpredictable. The most effective and efficient engagement and marketing programmes always learn from the successes of previous campaigns: evaluation is part of that learning. Evaluation of current engagement activity is the starting point in the next round of engagement planning.

These are some of the important criteria that can be used to judge qualitative or quantitative success:

- *Effectiveness*. How well did you achieve what you set out to achieve?
- *Efficiency*. How well did you use your resources in pursuit of your goals?
- *Benefits*. What can you point to as achievements and positive changes, either planned or accidental, as a result of your engagement programme and campaigns?
- *Costs*. What were the costs of the engagement programme and its overall value for money?

One way to structure your evaluation is to reflect on the processes that deliver or contribute to change over time:

- *outputs*: what you do
- *outcomes*: what happens as a result, what did they do, feel, sense, think, value or understand
- *ultimate impacts*: the long-term effect of change.

As many outcomes from engagement activities can be medium to long term it is not always easy to measure them, and more difficult to measure impacts. A good evaluation system and report includes stories as well as statistics. Statistics are particularly appropriate in measuring efficiency; stories of individual engagement help convey changes of attitudes or other qualitative changes in response to the library and its offers.

Outputs are usually tangible products, and are relatively easy to monitor and count. You can create ongoing procedures to collect and report this data. Examples of countable outputs for a library engagement programme include:

- online activity including websites, tweets and blog posts
- exhibitions
- publications including leaflets, articles and reports
- partnerships
- training courses
- participants and audiences for library events.

Measuring 'reach' (the estimated number of potential unique users or other stakeholders who could see your engagement campaign materials) and the number of 'impressions' (how often your content has been displayed on a screen or otherwise been made available to be seen by a user) can be very useful output indicators, especially where your engagement activities focus on achieving broad awareness rather than simply influencing a few key stakeholders. Be aware that calculating reach does not tell you how many people actually see or notice your engagement activity but rather the potential number who might do so. A measurement of reach is often accompanied by a measure of frequency: not simply how many potential users you have contacted but also how many times they are likely to have seen your message.

While outputs are relatively easy to capture and measure it is much more difficult to be confident of outcomes and impacts, which by their very nature can be significantly longer term. Outcomes for a library engagement programme include:

■ increased understanding of the library and the opportunities it offers
■ fun and general enjoyment
■ skills development
■ attitudinal change towards the library
■ inspiration and creativity
■ new experiences.

Longer-term impacts can be categorised into these three types:

■ *intellectual*: changes to how people think about the library, e.g. in awareness of the library and its services, understanding of what the library does, and development of positive attitudes towards the library and its services
■ *activity*: changes in what people do, e.g. skills development or participation
■ *organisational*: changes in how things work, e.g. to stakeholders' policies, behaviour or practices.

Evaluation criteria differ depending on your definition of engagement and the main drivers for your relevant activities: marketing campaign, planning, outreach, advocacy, customer experience and service, external relations. Marketing campaign objectives are likely to be quantitative, e.g. to generate more issues, visits or social media responses. Advocacy objectives are likely to be measured by more qualitative indicators, e.g. noticeable change of attitude or levels of support. User experience and service drivers are likely to be measured by a combination of quantitative and qualitative indicators, e.g. higher scoring in satisfaction surveys and greater general engagement through user experience management. In addition to campaign marketing and advocacy indicators and measures you may have outreach and external relations activities under your broad engagement plan and these too need some evaluation indicators and measures. There is no one dominant indicator to use and all indicators should be clearly related to the outcomes and impacts you seek from engagement.

There are specific indicators you can choose from for various engagement objectives. Marketing campaign planning engagement indicators include:

- website shares, clicks, likes, follows
- whether people are moving to your website from social media and what they are doing when they get there
- whether they are doing what you would like them to do.

Outreach engagement awareness indicators include:

- volume
- reach
- amplification (how far your message is spreading).

Advocacy engagement indicators include:

- the number of supporters or allies, e.g. in academic settings support from faculty, student groups, deans and chairs, and institutional administrators
- the number of opponents, in academic settings perhaps drawn from the same groups identified above
- noticeable change in the political climate, e.g. a change in the university's overall funding or tuition model creates opportunities for the library to discuss the question of library funding
- noticeable progress with decision-makers: are they more willing to listen to the library's position?
- an increase in the number of library staff who are aware of, and understand, the library's advocacy position.

User experience and satisfaction indicators include:

- *A user satisfaction score*. This derives from answers to questions beginning, 'How would you rate your experience with . . . ?' Users then rate their experience on a point from 'very satisfied' to 'very unsatisfied', usually measured on a five- or seven-point scale.
- *A net promoter score*. This is calculated from the likelihood of a user referring an organisation (your library) to someone else. The value of a net promoter score is that it is not simply about the emotion of being satisfied or otherwise but rather about the action of putting an organisation's reputation on the line. Take the percentage of 'promoters' (9–10 on a ten-point scale) and subtract the percentage of

'detractors' (0–6 on a ten-point scale). The 'passives' score 7–8 and are not part of the overall calculation. You can build this into e-mail surveys through www.trustfuel.com or www.promoter.io.

- *A user effort score*. This is calculated from measuring answers to a single question such as, 'Did the library make it easy for you to handle your issue?', usually measured on a five- or seven-point scale.
- *Unobtrusive testing or mystery shopping*. Potential user experience issues can be anticipated if the library tests unobtrusively that its services are indeed being delivered as promised and intended. The results of such a test can identify improvements required to library processes, identify areas for staff training and shake managerial complacency. Public libraries have used mystery shopping to evaluate a very wide range of things including first impressions, friendliness, helpfulness, quality of response to reference and telephone enquiries, and the physical appearance of the library.

There are ways to evaluate user experience and satisfaction less formally:

- Use the website to answer a question about the library. Was it easy or difficult? Were you frustrated? Did you get the answer you sought? If it takes you only a couple of minutes to get your answer or resolve your issue online user experience is likely to be at least acceptable. If it takes more than a couple of minutes to find the required information or resolve the issue then take a closer look at the process, the functionality of your website modules, and, most importantly, the feedback you receive from your users.
- Think about your staff, particularly those who are part of frontline teams. Do they need training? Are they polite and supportive of users? Are they engaged or disengaged?
- Ask your staff what complaints they get from users. Discuss how reasonable these complaints are and how to respond to them.
- Follow a query through and consider library processes. Are they all necessary or do some not add any great value for users? Do some not only add unnecessary complication but positively irritate users?

These are some external relations indicators:

- the degree to which your library networks and shares, nationally and internationally
- the quality, and perhaps number, of contacts your library has with influencers and decision-makers

- the degree of direct access your library has to engage policy-makers in dialogue and consultation processes
- how well your library is perceived to be good value for money by relevant stakeholders
- the level of exposure your library has to potential funding sources
- the degree to which your library's mission and vision are clearly understood by the stakeholders
- the amount of media interest in the library.

It is unlikely that you will include all these indicators in your approach to evaluation and, indeed, your circumstances may suggest you use other indicators. Make sure any evaluation programme is crisp, clear and useful. At its most basic simply ask yourself after every engagement campaign:

- Did it achieve the goals it set out to meet?
- What worked especially well?
- What didn't work quite as well as hoped?
- If we were to start this again what would we do differently?
- What should be done exactly the same next time?

It can sometimes be difficult to evaluate library awareness campaigns as they can be seen as a success even if issues, visits or enquiries do not immediately increase. Many companies carry out pre- and post-advertising surveys of awareness to identify a baseline and outcome measures. However, most library systems do not have the resources to undertake such detailed evaluation.

Certain library engagement and marketing activities are more easily evaluated than others. Campaigns that focus on drawing visitors to the website have a natural counting mechanism in the visitor log built into most systems. For this reason it might be useful to direct most of the promotional campaigns via the website, particularly those aimed at the more computer literate segments of the library market.

Evaluating engagement outcomes from social media presence and participation

One advantage of using social media in an engagement plan is that a social media presence increases activity, and makes it possible to monitor sentiment towards the library service. There have recently been concerns that traditional indicators such as counts of library activities have limited use, and social listening is becoming a key engagement activity.

Do not become obsessive about numbers and exact measurement. Sometimes libraries have been known to be so obsessed with large numbers of likes and shares that they have campaigned mutually to like and share each other's social media posts. This is clearly not the purpose of engagement. However, it does pump prime potential users. Who wants to be the first to like, share or comment on a social media post?

These are some potential digital media activities that could usefully be evaluated:

- audience growth rate of followers
- active engagement, including user comments, retweets and post shares
- clicks on links per post
- amount of user-generated content, e.g. user posts
- audience demographics, e.g. Twitter analysis
- mentions on other accounts
- likes, which are not as revealing as 'shares' but may still be worth counting.

There is now a large range of social media monitoring and management tools such as Agorapulse, Buffer, Hootsuite, Keyhole, Kissmetrics and Oktopost. Do not forget that Facebook, Google and Twitter have analytics you can access. Given the nature of the speed of change in social media it is highly likely that some of these will be modified or disappear and others take their place.

Social media is at its most useful when it allows you to have an ongoing conversation with your library users and other stakeholders. You cannot be a good conversationalist if you are not paying attention to what your users are most excited to talk about. This is reflected in the wider social media evaluation world by a move away from simply counting likes towards more social listening.

The library should not simply listen, though, but encourage user-generated content of posts and user photos. This helps with establishing that the library or information service is a good thing to be associated with (its 'social proof'). The library should reflect on and evaluate its social proof as evidenced by one or more of the following perceptions:

- The library or information service is truly expert and known to be by those you wish to engage with or their friends.
- Celebrities respected by those you choose to engage with offer positive messages about libraries.
- Existing users and key stakeholders have no hesitation in recommending the library to their friends or contacts.

■ An external body respected by those you wish to engage with bestows its seal of approval or certification on the library.
■ Large numbers comment on or share your posts. Likes and follows are less social proof but may be worth reporting.

Many metrics can be used to evaluate the library website. These focus on engagement aspects: bounce rate, average time on page, average session time, scroll depth, returning users, number of shares, number of comments. The first four provide a good indication of whether your content and general usability is well matched to needs and the latter two provide important indicators of how deeply engaged users are.

Evaluating employee engagement

As noted earlier in this book, user and other external stakeholder engagement is underpinned by the need for at least good, if not outstanding, employee engagement. If employees are unhappy in their work and do not promote the library vision and values then how will users, potential users and other external stakeholders be drawn closer to the library and its services? Engaged employees are more willing to go the extra mile and provide a very significant input into the success or otherwise of the library service.

There is no one agreed definition or measure of employee engagement. Define your own relevant construct to measure. Consider whether you are evaluating:

■ a psychological state
■ a combination of attitudinal and behavioural characteristics
■ general satisfaction with employees' work environment and employment relations practice.

Most organisations evaluate employee engagement by psychological state. The Utrecht Work Engagement Scale is the most prevalent measure in use. It offers four indicators on a real-time dashboard:

■ *Employee engagement*. How engaged are employees with their job?
■ *Absorption*. To what extent does employees' work thrill them, and to what extent do they forget about other issues while working? Absorption also measures the extent to which employees concentrate on their job and how it affects them personally.
■ *Dedication*. Are employees inspired in a job they think useful? Are they enthusiastic and proud of the work they do? Is it challenging enough?

■ *Vigour*. Do employees have adequate resilience and energy levels to deliver well? Can they persevere when the going gets difficult?

A word of caution on formal approaches to assessing employee engagement. Beware of looking for total work engagement – this only encourages behaviour that results in workaholics who may become 'burnt out'. Who is going to be engaged if confronted with an employee suffering burnout?

Reporting evaluations and assessments

By this stage of the process it is hoped that you can report on a successful engagement process and be keen to develop this further through follow-on programmes and campaigns. Celebrate your successes and use them to motivate your employees to even greater engagement.

To win support for your continuing commitment to engagement provide convincing evidence of the value in doing so through the end of programme or project report. Here is some guidance for writing an effective engagement programme evaluation report:

■ Ensure that you write the report with your programme objectives clearly in mind throughout. Keep referring back to them showing successful achievement where possible, but more likely evidence of movement along the longer route to meeting library objectives.
■ Tailor the report's content, format and style to the audiences you have for it, possibly modifying a core text for different sets of reader. Although this may seem to be time-consuming there are many benefits of such customisation. You do not want those reading the report to think it is irrelevant to them.
■ As with most reports be aware that not all of those who read it will want to read all of it. Communicate essential points by writing an impressive executive summary, which may be tailored to different audiences.
■ Describe essential features of the engagement programme, giving a clear explanation of the measures and indicators you have applied. If you feel that the audience will challenge any of them be careful to include the rationale and evidence to support your methodological choices.
■ Ensure there is a clear logic between the evidence and your judgements, outlining the limitations of the evidence.
■ Discuss next steps with their resource implications. This is your opportunity to turn your engagement programme into an ongoing programme developing the conversation with users, potential users and other stakeholders.

- Create a logical journey through the report, remove technical jargon and use examples, illustrations and graphics (e.g. infographics are a good way to communicate a mass of facts).
- Remember that your report is about engagement so you must be engaging in the style of your report. Without doubt the inclusion of real life stories, perhaps a side bar in the report, attracts readers much more than pages and pages of dense text interspersed with a few stock photos.
- Wherever possible discuss your report with your employees before finally signing it off and delivering it to appropriate people. How are you going to involve employees if they are only seen as a very minor part of the evaluation?
- If you are presenting the evaluation at a meeting of external stakeholders it is worth considering taking one or two of your engaged employees with you to present part of the report or to offer stories at the presentation.

Undoubtedly the reporting stage is unlikely to be the most exciting part of the whole programme, but if well managed it can be one of the most satisfying. Do not allow the reporting stage to be an uninspired end to the programme. Find appropriate ways within the team to celebrate your outcome and impact successes and move the programme further into a deeper engaging conversation with users, potential users and key stakeholders.

Complete Table 11.1 to set out your achievements and if possible identify some attention-grabbing features to use in your evaluation report. Use a combination of statistics and stories to summarise the success or otherwise of your engagement activities.

Table 11.1 *The outputs, outcomes and impact of different programmes*

Programme	Outputs	Outcomes	Impact

The final chapter offers some overall advice on how to help your programme deliver the rewards you seek.

12

How to give marketing and engagement the best chance of success

If you have reflected on the concepts, tools and techniques in the previous chapters you have the building blocks for effective engagement with the outputs, outcomes and impacts discussed in Chapter 11.

Your engagement programme will be a series of projects and campaigns where inevitably there will be surprises that constrain, or even derail, you from fulfilling your ambition. When you start your programme it is worth taking a little time to consider the risks inherent in it and consider mitigation possibilities. Although rarely seen as an exciting part of the programme, paying early attention to a risk management approach could ensure progress when the almost inevitable risks turn into programme difficulties. Consider the major things that may go wrong and assess their likelihood and consequences.

What if your major funding stakeholder suddenly changes? How will you manage any change of support for the programme? What if your programme assumes a motivated core team will deliver the programme and key members leave? What if the user experience turns out to fall short of your library promise? The one thing we know about planning is that things are unlikely to go to plan.

To give your strategies and initiatives the best chance of success here are 20 suggestions as you roll out your programme and campaigns:

1   Regardless of who writes the engagement plan, its efficacy comes from a wider internal team who deliver its promise and offer together. Ensure that these people talk to each other regularly and have a consistent message. They will get weary so inspire and motivate them. Celebrate your successes, even in small ways.

2   Engagement strategies and activities need support from external stakeholders. The library's governing body must share your vision and

give their commitment and support. Where appropriate ask for help and support from organisations such as the media. Similarly, although library staff frequently develop new skills be aware that you may need to seek outside help to implement some of your processes and activities. This can sometimes be difficult to achieve when budgets are tight.

3   Make sure there are no weak links in your engagement chain. Whatever the library offers is only as strong as the library's weakest link. Doing the right things needs to be accompanied by doing things right. To give your efforts the best chance of success the whole team must be committed and aware of the contribution they make in engaging stakeholders. A single instance of poor delivery of a promise could result in whoever was let down never using the library service again. This may have a multiplier effect if the potential user passes on negative comments, which discourage use by others.

4   Engagement is emotion-driven rather than simply information-driven. Keep your service 'human'. Telling users and potential users about what you have and what they can use in the library is unlikely to be engaging in itself. Make sure you present stories as well as facts.

5   Ensure sufficient time and skills are deployed to implement services effectively. Keep an item such as 'engagement activities' on the regular team meeting standing agenda. Without senior management buy-in engagement activities can be seen as unimportant rather than part of an ongoing series of linked projects in a programme that has a greater impact than the sum of its constituent projects.

6   Build confidence in your engagement strategy by aiming to achieve a series of quick wins to boost confidence. Beware making the job unnecessarily difficult by promising a service-wide revolution that inevitably does not deliver all its promise, confuses users and other stakeholders, and demoralises staff.

7   There must be real value in what you are doing for identified individuals, groups or organisations. You will not receive the desired attention and engagement if this value is not absolutely and abundantly clear to them as well as you. Communicate value relentlessly and make sure that those you wish to engage with are not left to work out for themselves exactly what the library is about.

8   If you are developing engagement activities to increase use rather than increase influence with funding and supporting bodies do not send messages about your products and services 'just in case they need them'. If you do not know that users need such messages and need them now then you are trying to educate them rather than market a service to them. Education is often accompanied by short-term

recollection of information followed by a gradual forgetting. Education is very useful for helping to build brand and influence perception but do not ever directly relate this to use levels in anything other than a very general way.

9   Synergies exist between engagement, advocacy, marketing, outreach, customer service and external relations. If each of these is seen as a separate responsibility then there is potential for a mismatch between strategy, action and outcomes. For instance, an appropriate marketing strategy to a particular segment may benefit from some advocacy background to amplify its effect. Once amplified it may not have the desired outcome if the delivery of the promise through customer experience and service is poor. On the other hand, a good marketing strategy supported by wider advocacy with a high level of customer experience and service satisfaction is likely to increase positive outcomes.

10   Make sure that there is an underlying consistent message between engagement, advocacy, marketing, outreach, customer service and external relations as they are closely connected. Libraries offer many products and services so make it easier for users and potential users to engage with them by issuing clear and simple messages. Once engaged the full splendour of the library can reveal itself to them. If messages are too complex they are not read by many recipients.

11   Library users will judge the library on their own experience not by what librarians have told them about it. This will influence how they describe the library to others. An effective engagement strategy is underpinned by consistent monitoring and development of user experience as people become engaged over a period.

12   Monitor user service to a very granular level. Every single interaction that users have with you and your service contributes to their image and perception of the library. It may take many good interactions to develop engagement but only one or two to derail that developing engagement.

13   Understand that engagement is not simply a series of facts but rather a set of perceptions and expectations that are either positive or negative, met or unmet. Users' expectations relate to their needs and what they think is realistically possible. What users and the library staff think is realistically possible may not align. Stay alert to this and its implications. Users' and other stakeholders' perceptions need to be managed.

14   Always check your marketing messages before sending them so the meaning is clear and recipients are likely to understand them in the manner you intend. Test them with a sample of appropriate recipients or, for very complex ideas (though try to avoid transmitting complex ideas by message if possible!), via a focus group.

15 Constantly seek feedback. If managed well this feedback will strengthen engagement as an early warning sign of disengagement and a source of new ideas to anticipate changing user needs.

16 Do not simply follow the advice of engagement gurus. Reflect on your own collection of data and build engagement strategies around what you have seen work for your users and other stakeholders. If you do not have the data, start to collect it now. Use outside recommendations for engagement strategies as small-scale experiments rather than hoped for game-changing new initiatives. Read widely and seek out success stories but have faith in your own judgement (no one should know your users and stakeholders better than you) to decide strategy and implementation activities. What worked elsewhere may not work for you and the initial comfort of seeming to follow best practice may quickly turn to disappointment and demoralisation.

17 Priorities matter. Do not get distracted from your tasks. In some organisational contexts funding appears to be a series of projects none of which is properly implemented and results in dissatisfaction. If engagement is a priority, prepare to defend your medium- to long-term plans as potential new initiatives may arise, which might lead some stakeholders to call for your resources to be repurposed.

18 Keep your engagement processes as simple as possible as they will then be less likely to fail or underperform. Try to manage uncertainty with a degree of flexibility in your activities – there are too many variables for you to control in search of perfect implementation.

19 Social media offers great opportunities for engagement but ensure that you understand why you will be seen as authentic and worthy of interest on these channels. Make clear to audiences what value the library offers them or they will see any communication as inauthentic.

20 Never forget the goals and value of the wider institution. Engage with them and you have a chance of gaining organisational support in your attempt to connect with your library community. Moving far from these goals is likely to undermine the very support you need to be successful.

Follow these suggestions to keep your engagement activities on track, and stay alert to innovation to make step changes in library services rather than simply continually improve the way you do things currently.

There are many highly engaging innovations that, although you may not want to copy them exactly, may inspire new visions and services in library activities:

- *The Human Library* (www.humanlibrary.org; 'We publish people as open books'), formed in 2000, now operates on six continents. It creates a special dialogue room, where taboo topics can be discussed openly and without condemnation.
- *The Library of Things* (www.libraryofthings.co.uk; 'Borrow useful things for your home, projects and adventures. Affordable. Convenient. Kinder to the planet') is essentially a rental organisation in London, which offers mainly household items and tracks how much landfill you have saved by renting instead of buying.
- *Little Free Library* (www.littlefreelibrary.org) is a non-profit organisation that builds community, inspires readers, and expands book access for all through a global network of volunteer-led little libraries.
- *Dolly Parton's Imagination Library* (www.imaginationlibrary.co.uk) is a book gifting programme that mails free, high-quality books to children from birth until they begin school, regardless of family income.

Engagement is an outcome from a winning combination of innovative strategic marketing, together with its related concepts of outreach, advocacy, customer service and external relations. In the first chapter of this book the following definition of strategic marketing for engagement was offered:

> An ongoing, engaging, meaningful conversation with users, potential users and other stakeholders to understand the appropriate configuration of valuable products and services which can then be moulded into mutually beneficial segment-specific winning offers that are subsequently communicated, implemented, evaluated and monitored.

It is hoped that now you have read the book the importance of each of the concepts embedded in the definition is clear. Check all your proposed engagement activities against it and if they do not contribute to the definition, challenge their ability to deliver any hoped for engagement.

Your motivation for reading this book was probably that you believe that users' and other stakeholders' engagement is key to developing attractive, successful and sustainable library services. It is very likely that you have been disappointed by the results of some of your previous efforts and joyful about the success of others. This book has broken engagement down into a number of key ideas, strategies and tasks and it is hoped that it has suggested some useful, practical ideas and activities to implement and encourage greater engagement success. Starting tomorrow.

References

BorrowBox, 2020, 'Our Vision', https://www.borrowbox.com/.

Carnegie UK Trust, 2015, *Ambition & Opportunity: a strategy for public libraries in Scotland 2015–2020*, https://scottishlibraries.org/media/1133/ambition-opportunity-scotlands-national-public-library-strategy.pdf.

DCMS, 2018, *Libraries Deliver: ambition for public libraries in England 2016 to 2021*, Libraries Taskforce, Department for Digital, Culture, Media & Sport, https://www.gov.uk/government/publications/libraries-deliver-ambition-for-public-libraries-in-england-2016-to-2021/libraries-deliver-ambition-for-public-libraries-in-england-2016-to-2021.

Drucker, Peter F., 2015, *Management Challenges for the 21st Century*, Routledge.

Facebook, [2021], 'Downham Market Library', https://m.facebook.com/pg/downhammarketlibrary/about/?ref=page_internal&mt_nav=0.

Health Education England, 2020, 'Library and Knowledge Services', https://www.hee.nhs.uk/our-work/library-knowledge-services.

Koninklijke Bibliotheek, 2018, *Working with Words: strategic plan of the Koninklijke Bibliotheek, National Library of the Netherlands 2019–2022*, https://www.kb.nl/sites/default/files/docs/kbnb_beleidsplan_eng_may_2019_def.pdf.

Statista, 2021, 'Number of daily active Facebook users worldwide as of 3rd quarter 2020', https://www.statista.com/statistics/346167/facebook-global-dau/.

Recommended reading

This book has outlined the principles of user and other stakeholder engagement with libraries. The following selected publications support the key ideas and processes presented in its chapters. Within their pages you will find extra ideas, tools and techniques concerning important elements of engagement. These include marketing, communication, creating value propositions, influencing and influencers, digital technologies and employee engagement. Successful marketing plans will be driven by a creative combination of these topics.

Bridger, Emma, 2018, *Employee Engagement: a practical introduction*, Kogan Page. ISBN: 9780749483517.

> All your attempts to engage users and other stakeholders will be undermined if you do not manage staff engagement. This book, endorsed by the Chartered Institute of Personnel and Development (CIPD), the UK professional body for HR and people development, outlines a highly reflective and practical way to achieve this.

Clayton, Mike, 2014, *The Influence Agenda: a systematic approach to aligning stakeholders in times of change*, Palgrave Macmillan. ISBN: 9781137355843.

> As noted regularly in the preceding chapters you will not be able to create effective engagement with library communities or governing and funding bodies without the support of a range of stakeholders. This practical guide will be a useful resource for those of you wishing to pursue this idea further.

Eyal, Nir, 2014, *Hooked: how to build habit-forming products*, Penguin. ISBN: 9781494277536.

> Forming the 'library habit' in people is a potential component of an engagement programme. This very readable and practical book offers

strategies for building habit-forming products in the private sector but is useful in any context.

Godin, Seth, 2005, *Purple Cow: transform your business by being remarkable*, Penguin. ISBN: 9780141016405.
The oldest book on this list but perhaps one of the most succinct in offering ideas on how to address one of the most difficult issues identified in the book you have just read – the fight for attention. Many examples from the private sector outline how organisations have made themselves remarkable. Although not written for libraries, it will spark ideas on how the library can make itself remarkable and potentially engaging.

Gould, Scott, 2017, *The Shape of Engagement: the art of building enduring connections with your customers, employees and communications*, self-published. ISBN: 9781976095153.
Less than 150 pages of very reasonably priced excellent wisdom on engagement. Highly practical, it offers a number of models to structure your programme. It presents the synergy between customers, employees and communities very well. Perhaps the first book anyone should buy and read on engagement.

Osterwalder, Alexander, 2014, *Value Proposition Design: how to create products and services customers want*, Wiley. ISBN: 9781118968055.
Your library needs a set of great value propositions. This highly practical book will take you through stages to create powerful value propositions that engage your users and other stakeholders.

Smith, P. R. and Zook, Ze, 2019, *Marketing Communications: integrating online and offline, customer engagement and digital technologies*, Kogan Page. ISBN: 9780749498641.
At almost 700 pages, this is not an introductory overview but useful to dip into for particular parts of the engagement process. The chapter headings, although not using the specific language of 'engagement', are all relevant to the library engagement journey, offering a useful sequence of ideas and, most importantly, make it clear how all the elements fit together. Very readable and certainly worth having to hand when devising your marketing messages and channel strategy.

Weber, Larry, 2019, *Authentic Marketing: how to capture hearts and minds through the power of purpose*, Wiley. ISBN 9781119513759.

> This book makes a clear and persuasive connection between organisational purpose and engagement. Despite being very much based upon the 'for profit' sector, much of this is easily adapted to a range of library contexts.

Yesiloglu, Sevil and Costello, Joyce, 2020, *Influencer Marketing: building brand communities and engagement*, Routledge. ISBN: 9780367338688.

> Very comprehensive look at the process of building 'influencers' into your engagement activities. This is a very delicate process for libraries and there is much to learn from this book. Although not meant as a short practical guide and occasionally feeling a little academic, this book offers a number of viewpoints and key learnings from a series of chapters written by experts.

And finally:

Journal of Library Outreach & Engagement, Illinois Open Publishing Network. https://iopn.library.illinois.edu/journals/jloe/index.

> A welcome addition to the list of library journals, Volume 1, Issue 1 appeared in 2020 with substantial articles and short notices on outreach and engagement in libraries. The first issue, which is freely available on the web, ran to over 100 pages and promises to be a good source of library engagement research and comment in the issues to come.

Index